lonely planet

VANCOUVER
ENCOUNTER

JOHN LEE

Vancouver Encounter

Published by Lonely Planet Publications Pty Ltd
ABN 36 005 607 983

Australia	Head Office, Locked Bag 1, Footscray, Vic 3011
	☎ 03 8379 8000 fax 03 8379 8111
	talk2us@lonelyplanet.com.au
USA	150 Linden St, Oakland, CA 94607
	☎ 510 250 6400
	toll free 800 275 8555
	fax 510 893 8572
	info@lonelyplanet.com
UK	2nd fl, 186 City Rd
	London EC1V 2NT
	☎ 020 7106 2100 fax 020 7106 2101
	go@lonelyplanet.co.uk

This title was commissioned in Lonely Planet's Oakland office and produced by: **Commissioning Editor** Jennye Garabaldi **Coordinating Editor** Evan Jones **Coordinating Cartographer** Marc Milinkovic **Layout Designer** Jacqui Saunders **Assisting Editor** Kim Hutchins **Assisting Cartographers** Amanda Sierp, David Kemp **Managing Editor** Brigitte Ellemor, Bruce Evans **Managing Cartographer** Adrian Persoglia, Alison Lyall **Cover** Image Research provided by lonelyplanetimages.com **Project Manager** Sarah Sloane **Managing Layout Designer** Sally Darmody **Thanks to** John Mazzocchi, Wayne Murphy, Michael Ruff

ISBN 978 1 74179 052 8

Printed through Colorcraft Ltd, Hong Kong.
Printed in China.

Acknowledgement Vancouver TransLink Map © 2009 TransLink

Mixed Sources
Product group from well-managed forests and other controlled sources
www.fsc.org Cert no. SGS-COC-005002
© 1996 Forest Stewardship Council

HOW TO USE THIS BOOK
Colour-Coding & Maps

Colour-coding is used for symbols on maps and in the text that they relate to (eg all eating venues on the maps and in the text are given a green knife and fork symbol). Each neighborhood also gets its own colour, and this is used down the edge of the page and throughout that neighborhood section.

Shaded yellow areas on the maps denote 'areas of interest' – for their historical significance, their attractive architecture or their great bars and restaurants. We encourage you to head to these areas and just start exploring!

JOHN LEE

Born in the near-London English city of St Albans, John decamped to Canada at the first opportunity after getting his undergrad degree to study an MA at the University of Victoria, British Columbia. Soon realizing his thesis on William Morris wasn't going to launch him along an obvious career path, he headed to Tokyo to teach English as a second language before jumping on the Trans-Siberian Railway for a long think. After two days, he was struck by the novel idea of becoming a travel writer and eventually launched a determined, if not exactly lucrative, full-time freelance writing career. Ten years later, now living in downtown Vancouver, he's still doing it. John's travels have taken him from Seoul to Reykjavík and deepest Texas (not on the same trip) and his stories – many of which seem to involve beer – have appeared in more than 150 publications around the world. Check his latest epic at www.johnleewriter.com.

JOHN'S THANKS

Thanks to Jennye at Lonely Planet for inviting me to work on this project, arguably the most enjoyable LP book I've ever written. I'd also be remiss if I didn't thank my friends and family on the West Coast for allowing me to not-so-subtly pick their brains for ideas.

THE PHOTOGRAPHER

Christopher Herwig was born and raised in Surrey BC. After graduating with a photography diploma, he spent several years traveling and photographing throughout Africa, Asia, Europe, Australia and Central America. In between trips he worked in commercial photo studios in London, Stockholm and Vancouver. After doing freelance work in Kazakhstan and Monrovia, Christopher is currently on a home break in Vancouver. His work can be seen at www.herwigphoto.com.

Cover photograph Boats moored at Jericho Beach marina, Vancouver, Photolibrary/Radius Images. **Internal photographs** p43, p72, p96 by John Lee; p16, p26, p27 Gunter Marx/Alamy; p23 Jason Kwan/Alamy; p132 Photo Bliss/Alamy; p148 Interface Images - Human Interest/Alamy. All other photographs by Lonely Planet Images, and by Christopher Herwig except p18 Richard Cummins; p20 Ray Laskowitz; p24 Doug McKinlay; p123 Glenn van der Knijff; p4, p10, p19, p44, p69, p79, p81, p86, p103, p120, p151 Lawrence Worcester.

All images are copyright of the photographers unless otherwise indicated. Many of the images in this guide are available for licensing from **Lonely Planet Images:** www.lonelyplanetimages.com

A photogenic totem pole at Brockton Point (p58) in Stanley Park welcomes the visitor

CONTENTS

Why is our travel information the best in the world? It's simple: our authors are passionate, dedicated travelers. They don't take freebies in exchange for positive coverage so you can be sure the advice you're given is impartial. They travel widely to all the popular spots, and off the beaten track. They don't research using just the internet or phone. They discover new places not included in any other guidebook. They personally visit thousands of hotels, restaurants, palaces, trails, galleries, temples and more. They speak with dozens of locals every day to make sure you get the kind of insider knowledge only a local could tell you. They take pride in getting all the details right, and in telling it how it is. Think you can do it? Find out how at **lonelyplanet.com**.

THIS IS VANCOUVER

You can always spot first-time Vancouver visitors. They're the ones suddenly rooted to the spot after glimpsing a gleaming snowcapped crag perfectly framed between a pair of shiny downtown towers. It's a signature city view that even locals rarely take for granted.

It's also a reminder that jaw-dropping nature is the main lure of this verdant metropolis. Stroll to the tip of Canada Place for the full effect: you'll find broccoli-green Stanley Park winking on your left; the shimmering waters of Burrard Inlet rippled by plunging floatplanes ahead; and that looming wall of jagged mountains framing the panoramic skyline.

But while this grand backdrop supplies stirring visuals for the 2010 Olympic and Paralympic Winter Games – the city's biggest-ever sporting fiesta – there's much more to Vancouver than good looks. And even if you miss the five rings rolling in, it's worth poking beneath this dazzling exterior to find out what really makes the place tick.

You'll find an easily explorable city divided into bite-sized neighborhoods, each with a different personality. Downtown is the mainstream hub of shops and crowds; Gastown is the cobbled historic home of great bars; Chinatown is the kaleidoscope of exotic stores and eateries; Kitsilano is the laid-back, beachside stretch of clapboard heritage homes; Commercial Drive is the boho enclave of counter-culture cool; SoMa is the capital of trendy hipsterism; and the West End is the out-and-proud 'gayborhood.'

As you wander around these urban haunts, British Columbia's natural treasures will be continually calling to you. So join the locals and go with the outdoorsy flow. You'll never forget kayaking at sunset on the glassy waters off Jericho Beach, doing sigh-triggering cycling treks around Stanley Park's picture-perfect seawall, and the time you made your bid for Olympic skiing glory on those alluring edge-of-the-city slopes.

Top left 'Killer Whale' sculpture by Bill Reid at the front entrance to the Vancouver Aquarium (p60) **Top right** If he can do it, you can; crossing Capilano Suspension Bridge (p53), spanning the Capilano Canyon **Bottom** The Museum of Vancouver (p111), at night

Vancouver reveals itself from behind the clouds of snowcovered Grouse Mountain (p61) at sunrise

HIGHLIGHTS

>1 STANLEY PARK

WEAVE THE SEAWALL AND SIGHTS IN VANCOUVER'S FAVORITE OUTDOOR HAUNT

Energetic visitors like to take in the entire 8.8km seawall in Stanley Park (p56), but there's much more to this spectacular urban oasis than its breathtaking, vista-hogging perimeter promenade.

That said, there are few better ways to spend an afternoon in Vancouver than joining the cyclists, wild-eyed rollerbladers and huffing, sweat-soaked joggers for a wind-whipped stroll defined by sea-to-mountain panoramas on one side and dense, gently rustling trees on the other. And if you're wondering how to tell the locals from the tourists, the Vancouverites are the ones who don't bat an eyelid at any of this as they barrel past.

If you don't have the time or the steel-like calves to go the whole hog, or if you're just craving a swift taste of what's on offer, the dense park is also stuffed with enough attractions to keep just about anyone happily occupied. You'll find hyped-up kids making a beeline for a trundle on the Miniature Railway (p59), closely followed by an excited run to the adjoining Children's Farmyard (p59) to tug the ears of rabbits and outstare the llama (he always wins).

Nearby is the granddaddy of all the park's attractions. The hugely popular Vancouver Aquarium (p60) isn't just for kids: anyone can

stare mesmerized at the alien iridescent jellyfish then watch the playful otters that always look like they're just about to start chuckling.

No matter where you're from, the park always does a good job of slowing down your heart rate and making you sigh deeply. It's the overwhelming nature fix that triggers this restorative response, especially if you hit Second Beach (p59) or Third Beach (p63) in the evening for the kind of spectacular ocean sunset that's guaranteed to make you fall instantly in love with Mother Nature.

She'll also be in your thoughts if you stroll around the tranquil, tree-lined trail encircling Lost Lagoon (p59). The traffic clamor from the nearby highway quickly dissolves away as you amble along the northern bank, keeping your eyes peeled on the water for bustling ducks, imperious swans and an occasional meter-high blue heron standing stock-still just off the shoreline. Nip into the Lost Lagoon Nature House (p59) on the south bank for a chat with the experts.

And before you go, spare a smile for the man whose moniker graces the park. One of several off-the-beaten-path statues (p59), the bronze figure of Lord Stanley nestles in the trees with its arms outstretched. On the plinth is a legend he uttered on the park's official opening day: 'To the use and enjoyment of people of all colours, creeds and customs for all time.'

See p56 for more on Stanley Park.

>2 ARTSY GRANVILLE ISLAND

HIT THE ARTISAN TRAIL ON A CRAFTY ISLAND STROLL

Originally an industrial enclave built on a pair of man-made sand-banks, Granville Island (p92) has come a long way since grungy little factories crowded its labyrinthine alleyways. Many of the old sheds are still in place but they're now colonized by independent galleries and artisan studios, as well as shops, theaters and eateries. In fact, the place where Vancouver's hardest workers once toiled has become a leisure-lover's utopia and one of the city's best and most relaxing half-day hangouts.

Artsy types should peruse the galleries lining both sides of Cartwright St near the intersection with Old Bridge St. Dodge the slow-moving cars searching for parking spots and you'll find glass-blowers, jewelry-makers and the excellent Gallery of BC Ceramics (p95), showcasing everything from abstract pottery to reasonably priced painted mugs.

Just around the corner, Railspur Alley is a hidden backstreet named after the old train line that's still embedded in its sidewalk.

The eclectic stores here include cool sake- and hat-makers and the Agro Café (p97), a friendly coffee shop where artisans rub shoulders with shoppers. Grab a perch on the breeze-licked patio if the weather is amenable and consider an organic ale alternative to a cup of joe.

Hopefully, you'll be fairly lost by this stage, which is always the best way to experience the island (if you fall into the water, you've walked too far). Keep exploring among the sheds and alleys – expect to find a few smiling artisans grinning at you as your peer through windows – then follow the students to Emily Carr University (p94) for its free-entry gallery.

Try to find the clutch of handsome houseboats bobbing gently a few steps north from here (make an offer if you're tempted to move in) or head in the opposite direction and join the shopping crowds along Johnston St. On your left will be the Net Loft building, lined with tempting little shops such as Paper-Ya (p97). If it's time to nosh, the clamorous covered Public Market (p97) is on your right. Lined with pyramids of produce, snack-happy deli stands and a cornucopia of craft and food stalls, it's an ideal browse-lover's hangout.

>3 GASTOWN BARS

DRINK, DRINK AND BE MERRY IN THE CITY'S BEST CHARACTER BARS

It's hard to look at 'Gassy' Jack Deighton's sprightly statue perched atop a whiskey barrel in Maple Tree Sq without feeling a little thirsty. Luckily, since you're in the heart of historic, cobble-streeted Gastown (p64), you'll be spoiled for choice over where to wet your whistle.

Modern-day Vancouver began when Deighton opened his first bar here, but the downtown core moved away a few decades later and Gastown sank into a protracted decline. Only recently has it been revitalized and its heritage of fabulous, century-old character build-ings is now colonized by the city's best watering holes, making this Vancouver's pub-crawl central. Old Gassy would be proud.

The landmark Steamworks Brewing Company (p73), one of Vancouver's few brewpubs, is the main tenant of a building that looks like it was hewn from a single block of granite. Its windowless, subterranean bar is recommended (although it's easy to lose track of time and spend the whole evening here) and its Lions Gate Lager is a light and refreshing way to start the evening. Time your visit for the monthly Green Drinks event, when local ecotypes grab a beer and chat about their new hemp underpants.

Behind Gassy's statue, between Water St's century-old warehouses and artsy new shops, you'll find the often-overlooked Six Acres (p73), a quirky brick-lined inn where hipsters quaff choice beers. It's an ideal candlelit bar on a rainy night, so take your time perusing the giant beer selection covering several pages of a menu bound in an old hardback book cover.

Across the street is the spot many locals list as Vancouver's best bar. Usually clamorous with animated chatter, the Irish Heather (p70) is a narrow gastropub where the hearty food lures almost as many regulars as the booze. Pull up a small table in the trad bar (built using Guinness-barrel floorboards) or join the giant communal table on the other side where locals will likely be discoursing loudly on everything from the Canucks to the cost of the 2010 Olympics.

If you're still thirsty, stroll along Alexander St to the Alibi Room (p71), Vancouver's best bar for British Columbia microbrews. There

are usually 19 on-tap tipples here in a welcoming high-ceilinged tavern that's striped with rows of long tables. Don't drink all the available brews, but do chat with fellow imbibers for tips on where to quaff tomorrow: hair of the dog might suddenly seem like a very good idea.

HIGHLIGHTS

>4 WEST SIDE BEACHES

STROLL THE REGION'S RUSTIC SHORELINE STRETCHES

With a spare day on your hands and an urge to escape the downtown crowds, pack a picnic and nip over to the city's West Side for
a long but leisurely hike along the beach-studded shoreline. It's the
kind of richly immersive, nature-bound experience that will quickly
slow your heart rate and make you consider applying for Canadian
residency (this usually happens just after you spot your first eagle).

Start your beachcombing odyssey at the wide, sandy elbow
otherwise known as Kitsilano Beach Park (p111), where the laid-back,
health-crazed locals will be jogging the trails or sunning themselves
as if they have nothing better to do (the perfect West Coast attitude).
Consider inviting yourself in for a beach volleyball game or just perch
on one of the logs studding the sand to blink in the glassy ocean
panorama backed by downtown's shimmering glass towers and the
distant, snowcapped peaks of the North Shore. It's a seminal Vancou-

ver view and one that is hard to adequately capture on camera – don't let that stop you trying, though.

West of here (about 2km away), Jericho Beach Park (p110) is generally less crowded and relatively more tranquil – expect your knotted muscles to have magically untied themselves by this stage. The birdlife is more numerous here (there's also the possibility of some harbor seal sightings) and the downtown core will be winking far behind you like a distant mirage. You'll also spot a few giant tankers idling in the inlet, and if you're tempted to hit the briny, you can rent a kayak or try your hand at windsurfing (p115). Either way, you'll meet plenty of chatty sporty types and you might even catch a tan.

The shoreline trail continues west if you're up for a longer stroll. The swanky homes of Point Grey will be rising in steps to your left as you finally reach Spanish Banks (p120) on the northern edge of the University of British Columbia (UBC) campus. Keep in mind that the tree-lined waterfront view from here is almost unchanged from the time when early European explorers sailed in to check out the area.

>5 BARD ON THE BEACH

ENJOY SHAKESPEARE ALFRESCO, WITH A MOUNTAIN-SUNSET BACKDROP

If Shakespeare were alive today, he'd definitely be a West Coast surfer dude spending most of his time bumming around local beaches. Well maybe not, but Vancouver's annual Bard on the Beach festival (p25) catches a little of that spirit with a summer-long theatrical run that's one of the city's most successful arts events.

Colonizing a grassy nook in the center of Kitsilano's Vanier Park (p111), the festival's stripy tents house up to four productions throughout the run, usually three Shakespeare plays and one Shakespeare-related number (think Tom Stoppard's *Rosencrantz and Guildenstern Are Dead*, for example).

Under the creative guidance of twinkle-eyed festival head Christopher Gaze – a local luvvie (actor) legend – the professional, often critically acclaimed shows lure thousands of Vancouverites every summer (booking ahead is highly recommended). It's also a good idea to bring a sweater for chilly evenings.

Arrive at least an hour before curtain to queue and claim your unnumbered seat with a sticky note (stationery provided), then visit the snack counter for a glass of wine and the gift shop for that all-important Shakespeare action figure. You'll likely spot Gaze wandering around the audience. Then it's time to let the poetic couplets take hold, as a golden sunset slowly unfurls over the mountain landscape behind the stage: all's well that ends well, methinks.

>6 SOUTH MAIN'S HIPSTER SHOPS

POKE AROUND VANCOUVER'S BEST INDIE STORES WITH A KITSCH-COOL CROWD

While downtown has lots of chain stores, visitors with more-eclectic shopping tastes should head to Main St. Starting at SoMa's W 20th Ave intersection, you'll find browsable indie shops patronized (and staffed) by the city's cool and friendly young hipsters. It's an accessible and laid-back strip to spend time pretending you're a local – retro Pumas and antique horn-rimmed glasses might help your disguise.

If you're cool enough to wear 1970s suit jackets ironically, peruse the vintage racks at Front & Company (p78), then nip across the street for Lazy Susan's (p78) off-the-wall accessories: it's the kind of store where finding kitsch-perfect gifts is easy. It's also a good spot to chat about the local scene – staff will likely recommend the Biltmore Cabaret (p83).

Alternatively, go southward – checking out the artful sidewalk stencils – and drop by creaky-floored Twigg & Hottie (p80). Its independent Canadian designer clothes will tempt your credit card but you might have to restrict yourself to the bargain rack at the back.

Finally, save time for the area's best oddball shop. Studded with vintage typewriters, the quirky Regional Assembly of Text (p80) is aimed at slavering stationery nuts lured by Japanese journals, literary T-shirts and the monthly, highly sociable letter-writing club. It's a cool, postmodern reaction to the email age that defines SoMa.

See p76 for more on SoMa.

>7 INDEPENDENT COFFEE SHOPS

SIP THE CITY'S RICH JAVA FIXES

The first non-US Starbucks arrived in Vancouver in 1987, but while there are plenty of the ubiquitous chain's outlets dotted around the city, there are many great independent pit stops to top up your mug.

The traditional heartland of lip-smacking Vancouver coffee is Commercial Drive (p84), where generations of Italian immigrants highly prize their beverage-making. Among the best is Café Calabria (p89), where you'll be sitting among a kitsch crowd of classical stat-ues…unless you can snag a little table outside with the elderly Italian gents watching people on the bohemian street pass by. Not all the joints are run by expat Europeans: on the other side of the Drive, the austere, whitewashed interior of the Prado Café (p90) lures a hipster crowd with its rich roasts and free wi-fi.

Luckily, you don't have to travel across town for a great indie cup. In the heart of downtown, Mario's (p51) combines smooth and strong roasts with dodgy Italian pop music (luckily, it's a takeout); the West End's Melriche's (p51) is a cozy hangout with hearty baked treats; SoMa offers Gene Café (p83), where posing in a corner with an existentialist novel is de rigueur; and Granville Island's Agro Café (p97) serves fair-trade java with a side order of artsy locals.

>8 STREETS OF CHINATOWN

IMMERSE YOURSELF IN THE COUNTRY'S BEST CHINATOWN

Canada's largest Chinatown (p64) is a wanderable smorgasbord of visual treats, from the giant Millennium Gate (Map p65, B4) at W Pender and Taylor Sts to the pagoda-topped red telephone boxes and the streetlamps topped with coiling golden dragons. When you're wandering the area's arterial Pender, Keefer and Main Sts, make sure you look above shop level: some of the city's oldest buildings are still here and their upper floors have often barely changed in many decades.

The best time to hit the 'hood is on a weekend afternoon in summer, when you can wander among the apothecary shops and grocery stores fronted by piles of dried fish, unfamiliar fruits and the occasional bucket of live frogs, then stick around for the Chinatown Night Market (p67), when the streets come alive with dozens of kitschy stalls and steamy food stands. If you miss the market on your visit, just head to an area restaurant: you can't go wrong at Hon's Wun-Tun House (p70), where hearty, aromatic dishes come with a side order of Chinese chatter provided by the regulars.

>9 UNIVERSITY OF BRITISH COLUMBIA (UBC)

HEAD BACK TO SCHOOL FOR A MUSEUM, GARDENS AND HIDDEN ARTWORKS DAY

The giant UBC campus (p116) is surprisingly stuffed with visitor attractions. Once you've got over the fact that, yes, students do look incredibly young these days, wander the pedestrian-friendly main thoroughfares and you'll find intriguing public artworks (p119), the smashing Botanical Garden (p118) and the fascinating Nitobe Memorial Garden (p119).

But save time for the university's main draw. The magnificent Museum of Anthropology at UBC (p119) is Vancouver's best museum and, following its recent expansion and overhaul, it's the perfect spot to delve into First Nations culture and beyond: a guided tour is the best way to guarantee full immersion.

And if you're still here in the evening, drop by the impressive Chan Centre for the Performing Arts (p121). It's one of Vancouver's best classical-music auditoriums. Alternatively, hit the books in the library. Just kidding.

More information on UBC can be found on p116.

>VANCOUVER CALENDAR

Vancouver is a year-round festival city (p132) but several major events tend to hog the limelight. Summertime's International Jazz Festival and MusicFest Vancouver offer a bewildering array of live music and both create a party atmosphere in downtown by staging free outdoor performances. For theater fans, it's hard to beat the International Fringe Festival and the edgy Push event, while Bard on the Beach may be the best way to catch a Shakespeare play.

The website of Tourism Vancouver (www.tourismvancouver.com) has a round-up of the city's bigger events. Check the *Georgia Straight* (www.straight .com) for up-to-date listings on smaller cultural happenings.

A symphony of fire highlights the Celebration of Light (p25) fireworks at English Bay

JANUARY

Push

www.pushfestival.ca

A challenging and illuminating run of innovative theater, dance and music performed by close-to-the-edge artists from around the world. It's a good way to meet the local artsy set. From the third week of January.

FEBRUARY

Winterruption

www.winterruption.com

Granville Island's concerted attempt to pretend it's not winter with four days of music, theater and family-friendly fun. Starts third week of February.

MARCH

CelticFest Vancouver

www.celticfestvancouver.com

A four-day St Paddy's Day celebration, complete with toe-tapping live music, a large market on downtown's Granville St and a big parade...plus lots of green beer and dodgy fake accents. Won't be held in 2010 due to the Olympics.

Vancouver Playhouse International Wine Festival

www.playhousewinefest.com

One of North America's oldest and largest wine festivals colonizes six days in late March. Events — including tastings and galas — often sell out months in advance, so book ahead.

MAY

Vancouver International Children's Festival

www.childrensfestival.ca

Bristling with kid-friendly storytelling, performances and activities in a charming multitented Vanier Park (Kitsilano) venue. Expect to have your face painted. Held in mid-May.

Face painting, Vancouver Children's Festival (above)

JUNE

Bard on the Beach

www.bardonthebeach.org

This professional repertoire company performs four plays per season from June at its Vanier Park tent site. Watch the show while the sun sets over the mountains behind the stage. Book ahead.

Vancouver International Jazz Festival

www.coastaljazz.ca

The city's biggest music fiesta is staged at venues around the city over 10 days from mid- to late June. It combines superstar performances with plenty of free outdoor shows in Gastown, Yaletown and on Granville Island.

Car Free Vancouver

www.carfreevancouver.org

An increasingly popular day-long event in mid-June when the main strips of several city neighborhoods – in Kitsilano, the West End, SoMa and Commercial Drive – are given over to pedestrianized street parties of music, performance and food. Great way to pretend you're a local.

JULY

Canada Day

www.canadaplace.ca/canadaday

Held from 10am to 7pm on July 1 at Canada Place, it includes exhibits, food and live performances. Granville Island stages its own, smaller event. Expect flag-waving and maple-leaf face paintings.

Vancouver Folk Music Festival

www.thefestival.bc.ca

A three-day Jericho Beach weekend in mid-July, with outdoor folk and world-music performances. Past headliners range from Billy Bragg to Bruce Cockburn. Bring some lotion or sunblock and tan your hide in the sun.

Celebration of Light

www.celebration-of-light.com

A giant four-day fireworks extravaganza over English Bay, starting from the end of the month. Avoid the crazy West End bottleneck by joining the low-key throng at Vanier Park.

AUGUST

Powell Street Festival

www.powellstreetfestival.com

One of several international community festivals staged around Vancouver – look out for Greek, Taiwanese and Portuguese days too – this colorful East Vancouver fiesta celebrates the city's Japanese culture. Staged in early August.

Pride Week

www.vancouverpride.ca

From early August, this multiday carnival of gay-, lesbian- and bisexual-friendly fashion shows, gala parties and concerts peaks with Vancouver's largest street parade. You'll spot plenty of near-naked locals…including some you'll wish were fully clothed.

MusicFest Vancouver
www.musicfestvancouver.com
Long known as Festival Vancouver, this event is a smashing two-week showcase of choral, opera, classical, jazz and world music, performed indoors and outdoors by local and international artists. Starts early August.

Pacific National Exhibition
www.pne.bc.ca
A two-week traditional country fair with shows, music concerts and farm animals –

plus a kick-ass old roller coaster that'll rattle your fillings even if you don't have any. Don't leave without scoffing some hot mini donuts. From mid-August.

SEPTEMBER
Vancouver International Fringe Festival
www.vancouverfringe.com
This is a giant and highly popular 11-day showcase of madcap comedy and challenging theatrics at large, small and unconventional venues around Granville Island…including the mini ferries. Starts mid-September.

Grooving it at the Vancouver International Jazz Festival (p25)

The historic wooden roller coaster at Playland during the Pacific National Exhibition (opposite)

Vancouver Comedy Fest

www.vancouvercomedyfest.com

Ten days of rib-tickling mirth during mid-September, with Canadian and international acts hitting stages at venues across the city. Book ahead for headliners.

OCTOBER

Vancouver International Film Festival

www.viff.org

More accessible than its starry Toronto brother, this 16-day screening of Canadian and international movies, beginning early October, is one of the city's leading annual events. Book ahead.

Vancouver International Writers & Readers Festival

www.writersfest.bc.ca

Five days of literary shenanigans in mid-October, with local and international scribes turning up for readings, seminars, galas and public forums. Past faves have included Douglas Coupland and Margaret Atwood.

NOVEMBER

Eastside Culture Crawl
www.eastsideculturecrawl.com
Dozens of eclectic artists from Vancouver's Eastside open their studios to visitors for this three-day, late-November event. An ideal way to get to know what the local artsy types are doing.

DECEMBER

Santa Claus Parade
www.rogerssantaclausparade.com
Vancouver's other (and far less naughty) main parade is a recent addition but has quickly become a popular early-December treat. The parade goes down W Georgia St and turns right into Howe St, downtown. Wrap up, watch the colorful floats and wait until the big guy shows up – he's definitely the real deal.

A totem pole at the fascinating Museum of Anthropology at UBC (p119)

ITINERARIES

Vancouver's grid-like street system makes navigating easy and the following itineraries will not only help you plan a one- to three-day visit but also provide ideas for free stuff, late openings and things to do when it rains (which it will).

DAY ONE

Kick off your day with a hearty breakfast at Templeton (p50) then stroll to visit the Vancouver Art Gallery (p42). Continue along Howe St towards the mountains and water, then switch east along Water St to peruse old Gastown. Visit the shops and galleries, snap the landmark Steam Clock (p66) and stop for lunch at the Irish Heather (p70). Pick up the pace for a trawl around nearby Chinatown, then end your day in Yaletown with a seafood feast at Blue Water Café (p46).

DAY TWO

Make for Stanley Park, where you should consider renting some wheels at Spokes Bicycle Rental (p54), or simply wander the seawall to see the totem poles (p58). Next, visit Lost Lagoon (p59) and the Vancouver Aquarium (p60). Walk into West End to Denman St's Mr Pickwick's (p49) for a fish-and-chips lunch. Later, drive or bus to SoMa for a mid-afternoon wander among indie stores and cool coffee shops. End your day with cocktails and tasting plates at the Cascade Room (p82).

DAY THREE

Take the edge off your cocktail hangover with an organic breakfast at Granville Island's Agro Café (p97), then inhale some fresh air on a shops and artisan-studios stroll. From here, walk southwest to Broadway (W 9th Ave) and hop on a B-Line express bus to the University of British Columbia (UBC). Wander the campus pretending you're a student (the hangover probably helps), then hit the Museum of Anthropology at UBC (p119) for a colorful First Nations cultural immersion. Finally, relax on a log perch at Spanish Banks (p120), where you can catch a languid sunset.

Top The street view of the Irish Heather pub and restaurant (p70) in Gastown **Bottom** The Naam restaurant (p114) in Kitsilano is a favorite of many vegetarians

ITINERARIES

RAINY DAY

Canada's 'Wet Coast' metropolis has plenty of options for those regular liquid-sunshine days. Granville Island's covered Public Market (p97) is ideal for a rainy morning, and it's only a short dash to the nearby Granville Island Brewing (p94) for an afternoon tasting tour. The three museums (p110) in Vanier Park are close enough together to keep visitors relatively dry – take an umbrella for the run to the Vancouver Maritime Museum (p111), though. And if you're traveling with kids, Science World (p66) will keep them occupied the longest – plus there's an on-site movie theater if it's still raining. Finally, Gastown's bars (p71) are close together for a relatively dry (until you start drinking) pub crawl.

FOR FREE

There are plenty of freebie alternatives for visitors aiming to rein in their costs. If you're in Stanley Park, check out the totem poles (p58) and Lost Lagoon Nature House (p59). Then stroll southeast along the seawall to

A cruise ship docked by Canada Place (p42), which looks like a ship itself, in downtown

FORWARD PLANNING

Trips to Vancouver usually don't need too much planning – unless you're coming for the 2010 Olympic and Paralympic Winter Games, in which case turn immediately to the relevant chapter (p123) and start moving ASAP. The second most time-sensitive planning need is for those wanting to catch a National Hockey League Canucks hockey game (p55) – capacity crowds are common, so booking as far ahead as possible is recommended. The same applies to top-class visiting music acts (see www.ticketmaster.ca for listings).

Three weeks before you go Check the Vancouver Calendar (p23) for upcoming festivals. Note that some, including the Vancouver International Jazz Festival, Bard on the Beach, Vancouver International Film Festival and Vancouver International Fringe Festival are particularly hot tickets.

One week before you go Reserve a table at top city restaurants such as **Lumière** (p114), **Bishop's** (p113) and **West** (p106). Check *Georgia Straight* (www.straight.com) for upcoming events and peruse the blogs and reviews at *Scout Magazine* (www.scoutmagazine.ca) for the latest news and vibes.

One day before you go Book a half-price show for the next day through **Tickets Tonight** (www.ticketstonight.ca).

Canada Place (p42), where the jetty-like promenade is recommended. Inside, the kid-friendly Port Authority Interpretation Centre is also gratis. Chinatown visitors should consider the free park adjoining the Dr Sun Yat-Sen Classical Chinese Garden (p66). It features similar pond and pagoda attractions. On Granville Island, there's no charge for the gallery at Emily Carr University (p94). And while the Vancouver Art Gallery (p42) isn't technically free, it offers admission by donation after 5pm Tuesday.

LATE OPENING

Vancouver is not exactly a 24-hour city but there are several options if you feel like staying up past 8pm. The Vancouver Art Gallery (p42) opens to 9pm on Tuesday and Thursday, while its quarterly FUSE event rolls until 2am. Alternatively, late opening at the Museum of Anthropology at UBC (p119) is to 9pm Tuesday. If you're hungry for late-night nosh, Kitsilano's vegetarian Naam (p114) opens 24 hours, while chatty Bin 942 (p105) won't kick you out until 2am. And of course there are the bars and clubs of the Granville Strip (p50), many of which stay open into the early hours, especially on weekends.

Downtown (p38) as seen from the eastern end of the Granville Street Bridge

NEIGHBORHOODS

Like a totem pole with many faces, Vancouver comprises a clutch of intriguing and highly distinctive neighborhoods. Each is easily explorable and those not around the city center are accessible by transit services. This means that you can have a uniquely different day out depending on which direction you choose to take.

Since it's where most of the hotels are, many start their explorations in the heart of the matter. Centered on W Georgia and Granville Sts, bustling downtown Vancouver is crisscrossed with mainstream shops and restaurants. You're also rarely more than a short stroll from the waterfront if you want to escape the crowds. To the southeast, Soho-esque Yaletown offers former brick-built warehouses now colonized by chichi boutiques and eateries. And to the northwest, the West End is a residential enclave of heritage homes and Canada's largest 'gayborhood.'

Nestled against the West End, Stanley Park is defined by its breathtaking and scenic outdoorsy appeal. Take a few minutes' walk eastwards from downtown and you'll be in the city's most historic area. Gastown's landmark old buildings are filled with indie shops and great bars. Adjoining Chinatown is equally heritage-flavored.

Departing the center brings even more alternatives. To downtown's southwest, Granville Island's public market and artisan studios are seemingly everyone's favorite sunny-afternoon hangout, while nearby Kitsilano is idyllically flanked with rustic beaches. The adjoining South Granville and Fairview area offers strollable shops and galleries, and it's an easy trip from here to the University of British Columbia (UBC) for several surprising visitor attractions.

Finally, cool travelers should make for two additional 'hoods: SoMa is replete with independent hipster stores; while Commercial Drive is a counterculture enclave of patio eateries and great Italian coffee shops.

Now you know where to go, strap on the daypack and get moving.

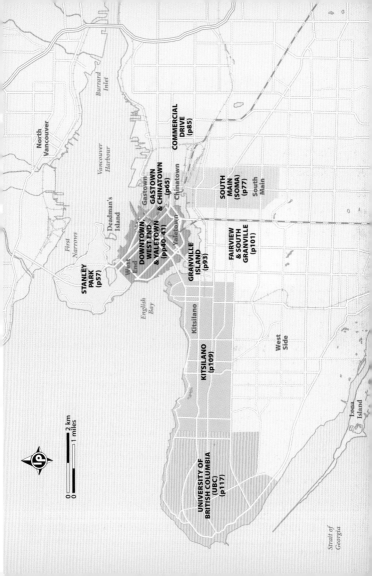

North Vancouver

Burrard Inlet

Vancouver Harbour

Deadman's Island

First Narrows

STANLEY PARK (p57)

West End

English Bay

DOWNTOWN, WEST END & YALETOWN (pp40–41)

GASTOWN (p65)

GASTOWN & CHINATOWN

Chinatown

COMMERCIAL DRIVE (p85)

Yaletown

GRANVILLE ISLAND (p93)

Kitsilano

SOUTH MAIN (SOMA) (p77)

South Main

FAIRVIEW & SOUTH GRANVILLE (p101)

West Side

KITSILANO (p109)

UNIVERSITY OF BRITISH COLUMBIA (UBC) (p117)

Logan Island

Strait of Georgia

0   2 km
0   1 miles

V

NEIGHBORHOODS

DOWNTOWN, WEST END & YALETOWN

>DOWNTOWN, WEST END & YALETOWN

Fringed by water and verdant Stanley Park, Vancouver's peninsular city center is crisscrossed with busy streets and forested with glass towers. Compact and highly strollable – gotta love that grid system – its heartland is the downtown core, where shopping and dining options abound.

DOWNTOWN, WEST END & YALETOWN

◉ SEE

Barclay Heritage Square ...	**1**	C3
BC Place Stadium	**2**	F6
BC Sports Hall of Fame & Museum	(see 2)	
Bill Reid Gallery of Northwest Coast Art ..	**3**	D4
Canada Place	**4**	F3
Coal Harbour Seawalk ..	**5**	E3
English Bay Beach	**6**	A3
Inukshuk	**7**	A4
Marine Building	**8**	E3
Port Authority Interpretation Centre	(see 4)	
Roedde House Museum ..	**9**	C3
Vancouver Art Gallery ...	**10**	D4
Water Park	**11**	D2

🏠 SHOP

Little Sisters Book & Art Emporium	**12**	B4
Lululemon Athletica ...	**13**	C4
Rubber Rainbow Condom Company ..	**14**	B2
Sophia Books	**15**	F4
True Value Vintage	**16**	D4
West End Farmers Market	**17**	C4

🍴 EAT

Blue Water Café & Raw Bar	**18**	D6
C Restaurant	**19**	B6
Chambar	**20**	F5
Glowbal Grill & Satay Bar	**21**	D6
Gorilla Food	**22**	F4
Guu With Garlic	**23**	B2
Japa Dog	**24**	D4
Joe Fortes Seafood & Chophouse	**25**	D4
La Bodega	**26**	C5
Le Gavroche	**27**	B2
Medina Café	(see 20)	
Motomachi Shokudo ...	**28**	B2
Mr Pickwick's	**29**	A3
Raincity Grill	**30**	A3
Templeton	**31**	D5

🍸 DRINK

1181	**32**	B4
Afterglow	(see 21)	
Dix BBQ & Brewery	**33**	E6
Fountainhead Pub	**34**	C5
Gallery Café	(see 10)	
Lennox Pub	**35**	D5
Mario's	**36**	E4
Melriche's	**37**	B4
Mill Marine Bistro	**38**	D2
O'Doul's	**39**	C3
PumpJack Pub	**40**	C4
Yaletown Brewing Company	**41**	D6

★ PLAY

BC Lions	(see 2)	
Caprice	**42**	D5
Celebrities	**43**	C5
CN Imax Theatre	**44**	F3
Commodore	**45**	D5
GM Place	**46**	F5
Media Club	**47**	F5
Odyssey	**48**	C5
Orpheum Theatre	**49**	D5
Pacific Cinémathèque ...	**50**	C5
Railway Club	**51**	E4
Spoke Bicycle Rental ..	**52**	B2
Tickets Tonight	**53**	C3
Vancity Theatre	**54**	D6
Vancouver Canucks ...	(see 46)	
Vancouver Playhouse ..	**55**	F5
Vancouver Symphony Orchestra	(see 49)	

Please see over for map

VANCOUVER >38

Downtown is flanked to the west by the primarily residential West End area, home to acres of heritage houses and Canada's largest gay district. On its southeastern flank is Yaletown, an historic brick-built warehouse area that's been reinvented as Vancouver's chichi Soho, complete with swanky bars and eateries. Wherever you wander, you'll find a diverse array of attractions, from art galleries to sports stadiums and architectural landmarks that will have you reaching for your camera (and wishing you had extra batteries). Fuel-up java and dining spots are on every corner and you'll find plenty of nightlife options including bars, theaters and live music.

◉ SEE

Eminently walkable, Vancouver's city center is studded with attractions for an on-foot day. And you're never far from a coffee or foodie pit stop.

◉ BC PLACE STADIUM

☎ 604-669-2300; www.bcplacestadium .com; 777 Pacific Blvd; Ⓜ Stadium
Venue for 2010's Olympic (p123) opening and closing ceremonies, Vancouver's biggest sports stadium also hosts the BC Lions football team (p52). Check out the **BC Sports Hall of Fame & Museum** (☎ 604-687-5520; www.bcsportshall offame.com; Gate A off Beatty St; adult/child $10/8; ⏱ 10am-5pm; ♿) for regional and national memorabilia plus its new Aboriginal Sport Gallery, then take a behind-the-scenes **stadium tour** (☎ 604-661-7362; Gate H; adult/child $8/5; ⏱ 11am & 1pm Tue mid-Jun–Aug).

◉ BILL REID GALLERY OF NORTHWEST COAST ART

☎ 604-682-3455; www.billreidgallery .ca; 639 Hornby St; adult/child $10/5; ⏱ 11am-5pm Wed-Sun; Ⓜ Burrard
Downtown's newest art space showcases carvings, paintings

Racing car at the BC Sports Hall of Fame & Museum (right), BC Place Stadium

400 m
0.2 miles

Vancouver
Harbour

Lost Lagoon

*Coal
Harbour*

Deadman's
Island

HMCS Discovery
Naval Training
Station

Royal Vancouver
Yacht Club

*Devonian
Harbour
Park*

Coal
Harbour
Quay

Coal Harbour
Park

Bayshore Dr

Harbour Green
Park

Canada Pl

Floatplane
Terminal

To Lonsdale
Quay

Waterfront Rd

SeaBus

Water St

Gastown

W Hastings St

W Cordova St

W Pender St

Dunsmuir St

See Gastown & Chinatown
Map p65

Tourist Information
Centre

Waterfront
Station

Vancouver Bullion
& Currency Exchange

Granville

Granville Mall

Vancouver
City Centre

Robson
Sq

Burrard

W Georgia St

Shangri-La
Tower

Melville St

Alberni St

Robson St

Haro St

Barclay St

Nelson
Park

Pendrell St

Comox St

Nicola St

Broughton St

Jervis St

Bute St

Thurlow St

West End

Barclay
Heritage Square

Star Internet
Café

Bidwell St

Cardero St

Denman St

Gilford St

Chilco St

Park Lane

Lagoon Dr

Bridle Path

See Stanley Park
Map p57

Beach Ave

English
Bay
Beach

W Pender St

W Cordova St

W Hastings St

Nelson St

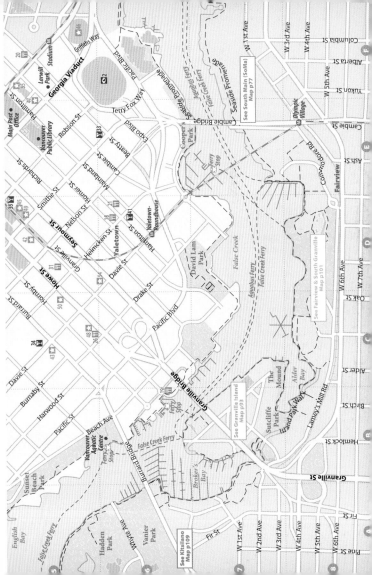

Griffiths Way

Larwill
Park

Georgia Viaduct

Hamilton St

35

20

Main Post
Office

Vancouver
Public Library

Robson St

Cambie St

Beatty St

Homer St

Mainland St

Hamilton St

Seymour St

Richards St

Nelson St

Smithe St

Davie St

Granville St

Howe St

Hornby St

Burrard St

Davie St

Burnaby St

Harwood St

Pacific St

Sunset
Beach
Park

English
Bay

False Creek Ferry

Ferry
Stop

Vancouver
Aquatic
Centre

Beach Ave

Maple Ave

Hadden
Park

Vanier
Park

Stadium

Pacific Blvd

Terry Fox Way

Expo Blvd

Pacific Blvd

Drake St

Drake St

Seaside Promenade

Seaside Promenade

Cooper's
Park

Yaletown-Roundhouse

Yaletown

David Lam
Park

False Creek

Aquabus Ferry
False Creek Ferry

Aquabus Ferry
False Creek Ferry

Granville Bridge

Ferry
Stop

Broker's
Bay

Burrard Bridge

Pine St

W 1st Ave

W 2nd Ave

W 3rd Ave

W 4th Ave

W 5th Ave

W 6th Ave

Fir St

Sutcliffe
Park

The
Mound

Alder
Bay

Island Park Walk

Lamey's Mill Rd

Hemlock St

Birch St

Alder St

Oak St

Ash St

Commodore Rd

Fairview

W 5th Ave

W 6th Ave

W 7th Ave

Cambie St

Cambie Bridge

Olympic
Village

Seaside Promenade

Aquabus Ferry
False Creek Ferry

Ferry
Stop

W 1st Ave

W 3rd Ave

W 4th Ave

W 5th Ave

Yukon St

Alberta St

Columbia St

See South Main (SoMa)
Map p77

See Fairview & South Granville
Map p101

See Granville Island
Map p93

See Kitsilano
Map p109

Granville St

33

54

31

49

35

42

50

34

43

48

26

19

18

21

41

46

2

and jewelry from Canada's most revered Haida artist. Lined with artifacts and touch screens, it's a comprehensive intro to Reid's work. Check out the Great Hall, then hit the mezzanine level: you'll be face-to-face with an 8.5m-long bronze of magical creatures, complete with impressively long tongues.

◉ CANADA PLACE
☎ 604-647-7390; www.canadaplace.ca; 999 Canada Place Way; Ⓜ Waterfront
Stroll the pier-like promenade alongside this sail-roofed landmark for breathtaking North Shore views, or duck inside for the **CN IMAX Theatre** (☎ 604-682-4629; www.imax.com /vancouver; 999 Canada Place; admission $12) and the hands-on, kid-friendly **Port Authority Interpretation Centre** (☎ 604-665-9179; admission free; ☷ 8am-5pm Mon-Fri, 10am-2pm Sat & Sun; ☖). The adjoining new convention center expansion has a grass-topped roof and a vista-hugging outdoor plaza.

◉ ENGLISH BAY BEACH
cnr Denman St & Beach Ave; ☒ 5
Wandering southwest along Denman St, you'll suddenly see palm trees rustling ahead of you, marking the fringes of Western Canada's best urban beach. There's a near-party atmosphere here in summer when West Enders hit the sand to catch the rays, play volleyball or peruse the artwork

vendors studding the waterfront. Be sure to check out the beach's towering *inukshuk* (Inuit sculpture) figure, a great sunset perch.

◉ ROEDDE HOUSE MUSEUM
☎ 604-684-7040; www.roeddehouse .org; 1415 Barclay St; admission $5; ☷ 1-4pm Tue-Fri, noon-5pm Sat, 2-4pm Sun; ☒ 5
A charming reminder of the well-to-do homes that once lined the West End, this 1893 clapboard house on Barclay Heritage Sq has been transformed into a period-evoking museum. The centerpiece of a string of attractive preserved piles in the area – nearby Barclay Manor is a favorite – it's brimming with antiques and friendly volunteers. Sunday entry includes tea and cookies for $1 extra.

◉ VANCOUVER ART GALLERY
☎ 604-662-4700; www.vanartgallery .bc.ca; 750 Hornby St; adult/youth/child $20.50/15/7, admission by donation after 5pm Tue; ☷ 10am-5:30pm Fri-Mon & Wed, 10am-9pm Tue & Thu; ☒ 5
The city's leading art space is a vibrant home for blockbuster visiting shows plus innovative exhibitions from its own collection – look out for photo conceptual art, a West Coast specialty. The hot ticket is to **FUSE** (admission $17.50), a quarterly late-night party with live performances, but also consider

Kathleen Ritter
Assistant curator, Vancouver Art Gallery

How many artworks does the gallery have? Almost 10,000, including the world's best Emily Carr collection and rich holdings of photo conceptualist work by Stan Douglas, Rodney Graham, Ian Wallace, Ken Lum and, of course, Jeff Wall. **What is FUSE?** It's a quarterly one-night event when the gallery space is activated with music, performance and cultural happenings in a celebratory atmosphere. It's also *the* place to see and be seen. **What else do artsy types do in this city?** Vancouver has a rich cultural scene with many galleries and artist-run centers. I go to lots of openings, music shows and cultural events. **Favorite festival** Push (p24). **Favorite live-music venue** Biltmore Cabaret (p83). **If you painted a Vancouver landscape, what would it be?** From Cambie Bridge overlooking the new Olympic Athletes' Village. It's a complete transformation of the area and represents all the challenges of a major city in development.

the gallery cafe's expansive patio – accessible to nongallery patrons, too. It's downtown's best alfresco coffee hangout.

🛍 SHOP

Lined with mainstream boutiques, Robson St is Vancouver's busiest shopping strip. Hipsters should also peruse the compact string of shops on Granville St between Robson and Smithe Sts.

🛍 LITTLE SISTERS BOOK & ART EMPORIUM *Bookshop*
☎ 604-669-1753; www.littlesisters.ca; 1238 Davie St; ⏰ 10am-11pm; 🚌 6
The center of the West End's bustling gay village, this popular store stocks a giant selection of specialist literature, has an active bulletin board and is staffed by a team of hyper-knowledgeable locals. A good stop for first-time visitors who want to check out the 'gayborhood' scene.

🛍 LULULEMON ATHLETICA
Clothing
☎ 604-681-3118; www.lululemon.com; 1148 Robson St; ⏰ 10am-9pm Mon-Sat, 11am-8pm Sun; 🚌 5
The flagship downtown store of the Vancouver-based chain that made ass-hugging yoga wear a mainstream fashion, this is the shop for that archetypal West Coast look. Sporty tops and pants

for ladies are the collection's backbone, but menswear is also part of the mix.

🛍 RUBBER RAINBOW CONDOM COMPANY *Condoms*
☎ 604-683-3423; 953 Denman St; ⏰ 11am-7pm; 🚌 5
Doing brisk West End business, this funky condom and lube store serves all manner of experiment-inviting accessories, including studded, vibrating and 'full-fitting strawberry flavored' varieties. Ask for a selection pack if you're going

The exterior of the Marine Building (opposite)

VANCOUVER'S ART DECO MASTERPIECE

Hugging the corner of W Hastings and Burrard Sts and once the tallest building in the British Empire, the 1930-built **Marine Building** is arguably downtown's most alluring heritage structure. The highlights of the 21-story tower include its detailed decorative exterior of seahorses, lobsters and streamlined steamships, but step into the lobby and you'll find a floor depicting signs of the zodiac, colorful stained-glass panels and sumptuously attractive etched elevator doors. Renovated in 1999, the structure is now an office building. If you're an art deco buff, also check out **City Hall** (p102) and peruse the website of **Heritage Vancouver** (www.heritagevancouver.org).

to be in town for a while – heck, you never know how lucky you might get.

🏠 **SOPHIA BOOKS** *Bookshop*
☎ 604-684-0484; www.sophiabooks.com; 450 W Hastings St; 🕑 9am-7pm Mon-Fri, 10am-7pm Sat, noon-6pm Sun; 🚌 4
Favored eclectic bookstore among in-the-know locals, Sophia's combines a strong selection of foreign-language books with a choice array of art, design and generally all-round-cool tomes. The manga comic books and the back wall of international magazines are highlights, especially among homesick English as a Second Language (ESL) students.

🏠 **TRUE VALUE VINTAGE** *Clothing*
☎ 604-685-5403; 710 Robson St; 🕑 11am-7pm Sun & Mon, 11am-8pm Tue, Wed & Sat, 11am-9pm Thu & Fri; 🚌 5
The used duds at this subterranean cave of kitsch-cool clothing

are sometimes pricey, but if you really need that 1950s bowling shirt or Jimi Hendrix tour hat you'll pay anything, right? Bargains – think John Deere T-shirts and hefty lumberjack jackets – are to be had on the musty-smelling sale racks.

🏠 **WEST END FARMERS MARKET** *Market*
☎ 604-879-3276; www.eatlocal.org; Nelson Park, btwn Bute & Thurlow Sts; 🕑 9am-2pm Sat mid-Jun–mid-Oct; 🚌 2
Hugging the south edge of little Nelson Park before a row of preserved heritage homes, this busy seasonal market is a popular locals' hangout. Arrive early for the best selection of fresh-picked, often organic fruits and veggies from regional farms (cherries, peaches, morels and heirloom tomatoes are recommended) and look out for extra treats such as piquant cheeses and delectable preserves.

NEIGHBORHOODS

DOWNTOWN, WEST END & YALETOWN

🍴 EAT

There are many restaurants above Robson St's shops, plus good contemporary Asian options at the street's Stanley Park end. Nearby Denman St is lined with international midrange options, while Yaletown is ideal for sophisticated, higher-end dining.

🍴 BLUE WATER CAFÉ & RAW BAR *Seafood* $$$
☎ 604-688-8078; www.bluewatercafe.net; 1095 Hamilton St; mains $22-44; 🕙 5pm-midnight; Ⓜ Yaletown-Roundhouse

For Yaletown's high-concept seafood restaurant, head straight to the semicircular raw bar and watch the chef's whirling blades preparing delectable sushi and sashimi. Alternatively, tuck yourself into a table at the warm, brick-lined dining room or chatty patio for perfectly executed West Coast mains such as sablefish, lingcod and arctic char.

🍴 C RESTAURANT *Seafood* $$$
☎ 604-681-1164; www.crestaurant.com; 1600 Howe St; mains $18-46; 🕙 11:30am-2:30pm Mon-Fri, 5:30-11pm daily; 🚌 C21

This pioneering fish and shellfish restaurant takes a revelatory approach to regional fare, combining simply prepared dishes such as

Lunchtime dining at the popular Templeton (p50) in downtown

side-stripe prawns and Queen Charlotte scallops with adventurous offerings including octopus bacon. Take your time and savor a long dinner or drop by for a good-value lunch.

CHAMBAR *International* $$$

☎ 604-879-7119; www.chambar.com; 562 Beatty St; mains $14-29; ⏱ 5:30pm-midnight; Ⓜ Stadium

A brick-lined, candlelit restaurant with a sophisticated European-influenced menu, favorites here include *moules et frites*, pan-seared scallops and a highly recommended tender lamb shank that makes velvet seem unyielding. Ideal spot for a romantic meal, next door's sister **Medina Café** (☎ 604-879-3114; www.medinacafe.com; 556 Beatty St; ⏱ 8am-5pm Tue-Fri, 9am-4pm Sat & Sun) is good if you're happy to have a cheaper date.

GLOWBAL GRILL & SATAY BAR *International* $$

☎ 604-602-0835; www.glowbalgrill .com; 1079 Mainland St; mains $16-26; ⏱ 11:30am-midnight Mon-Fri, 10:30am-midnight Sat & Sun; Ⓜ Yaletown-Roundhouse

This hip but unpretentious Yaletown eatery has a comfortable, lounge-like feel and a menu fusing West Coast ingredients with Asian and Mediterranean flourishes. The cheese tortellini

BANKSY BEWARE

Check out the work of Vancouver's best graffitos on the stretch of Beatty St between Dunsmuir and W Georgia (Map pp40–1, F5). Looking like an alfresco art gallery, the strip's western side has been sanctioned and preserved as an eye-popping exhibition of stunning street art. You'll find giant and kaleidoscopically colorful manga epics, sci-fi cityscapes and the incongruous appearance of stylized characters from the Flintstones and Peanuts.

with smoked chicken is ace, but save room for some finger-licking satay stick chasers – especially the tequila lamb, served with lime mint glaze.

GORILLA FOOD *Vegetarian* $

☎ 604-722-2504; www.gorillafood.com; 422 Richards St; mains $4-8; ⏱ 11am-5pm; Ⓥ ; 🚇 5

More guerrilla than gorilla, this subterranean downtown spot is perfect for raw-food devotes. Mimicking the diet of its namesake, nothing is cooked, which leads to innovative dishes such as crunchy lasagna (strips of zucchini substitute for pasta) and a pizza made from seed crust and topped with tomato sauce, tenderized zucchini and mashed avocado. Save room for an icy almond shake.

🍴 GUU WITH GARLIC

Japanese $$

☎ 604-685-8678; www.guu-izakaya
.com; 1689 Robson St; small plates $4-9;
🕐 5:30pm-midnight; 🚌 5

One of many highlight Asian
bistros at Robson St's West End
tip, you'll be chilling with the
ESL students as you pile up the
tasting plates here. Try black cod
with miso mayo or pork cheek
with ponzo sauce, plus an Asahi
Super Dry. With a seat at the
bar, watch the overworked chefs
meeting their spiraling whirlwind
of orders.

🍴 JAPA DOG *Comfort Food,*
Japanese $

www.japadog.com; cnr Burrard & Smithe
Sts; mains $4.50-6; 🕐 noon-7:30pm
Mon-Thu, noon-8pm Fri & Sat, 12:30-7pm
Sun; 🚌 2

Vancouver's best hotdog stand
eschews tasteless rubber wieners
for a fusion Japanese approach,
including the Misomayo, a turkey
smokie with miso sauce, and the
Terimayo, served with shreds of
nori. Arrive off-peak to avoid a
giant lunchtime queue and check
out the stand's gallery of oddball
famous patrons, including Steven
Segal and Ice Cube.

🍴 JOE FORTES SEAFOOD &
CHOPHOUSE *West Coast* $$

☎ 604-669-1940; www.joefortes.ca;
777 Thurlow St; mains $14-34; 🕐 11am-
11pm; 🚌 5

The heated rooftop patio is an
excellent spot to enjoy a West
Coast meat or seafood treat, ranging from slow-roasted prime rib
to miso-glazed halibut. The hearty
Cobb salad is recommended,
while shellfish fans shouldn't miss
the oyster bar. Look out for the
bargain $10 Blue Plate special
often available at lunchtime.

The atmospheric Raincity Grill (opposite)

🍴 LA BODEGA *Spanish* $$

☎ 604-684-8814; www.labodegavancouver.com; 1277 Howe St; plates $8-12; 🕑 4:30pm-midnight Mon-Fri, 5pm-midnight Sat, 5-11pm Sun; 🚌 10

An authentically rustic, off-the-beaten-path Spanish tapas spot, where ordering a jug of sangria and a pile of sharing plates is the way to go – be sure to include some hearty Spanish meatballs and spicy chorizo sausage. Weekend evenings generate a warm and welcoming atmosphere, so consider settling in for the night.

🍴 LE GAVROCHE *French* $$$

☎ 604-685-3924; www.legavroche.ca; 1616 Alberni St; mains $18-34; 🕑 5:30-11pm; 🚌 5

Another hidden gem, this heritage-house restaurant fuses West Coast ingredients with classic and contemporary French approaches. Employing *les fruits de mer* with practiced flair – check out the Alaska black cod with burnt orange and anise sauce – it's a good choice for a romantic fireside dinner. Wine-lovers take note: this place has a serious list.

🍴 MOTOMACHI SHOKUDO *Japanese* $$

☎ 604-609-0310; 740 Denman St; mains $8-14; 🕑 5-10pm; 🚌 5

Vancouver's best ramen house, this evocative little spot combines lightning-fast service with perfect comfort food. First-timers should try the new-generation miso ramen, brimming with (mostly organic) bean sprouts, sweet corn, shredded cabbage and barbecued pork. If the line-up's long, try its older sister noodlery a few doors south. Cash only.

🍴 MR PICKWICK'S *Comfort Food* $$

☎ 604-681-0631; www.mrpickwicks.bc.ca; 1007 Denman St; mains $8-13; 🕑 11:30am-9pm; 🚶 ; 🚌 6

The city's best fish-and-chippery knows exactly how to make your favorite comfort food – even the chips are chunkily satisfying. As well as the classics, the batter-fried salmon and crunchy crab cakes are excellent, while the house-made tartar and lemon dill sauces are perfect. Check daily specials and save room for a draft Dead Frog beer. Outstanding service.

🍴 RAINCITY GRILL *West Coast* $$$

☎ 604-685-7337; www.raincitygrill.com; 1193 Denman St; mains $20-30; 🕑 11:30am-2:30pm & 5-10pm Mon-Fri, 10:30am-2:30pm & 5-10-pm Sat & Sun; 🚌 5

A West End pioneer of seasonal regional ingredients, expect perfect dishes such as Fanny Bay oysters and Salt Spring Island lamb here. Popular features include the weekend brunch and daily three-course $30 tasting menu between 5pm and 6pm. The huge wine list is also a celebrated plus. If you're on foot, try the take-out window for a gourmet $10 sandwich.

🍽 TEMPLETON
Comfort Food $$
☎ 604-685-4612; 1087 Granville St; mains $6-12; ⏰ 9am-11pm Mon-Wed, 9am-1am Thu-Sun; 👶 ; 🚌 10
This funky 1930s diner serves organic burgers, fair-trade coffee and a great big-ass breakfast – the chicken quesadillas, served with lashings of salsa and sour cream, are also recommended. The mini jukeboxes on the tables don't work, so console yourself with a chocolate ice-cream float while spinning on your stool at the counter. Avoid weekend peak times or you'll be queuing forever.

🍸 DRINK
Downtown's Granville Strip, between Robson and Davie Sts, is lined with noisy bars and clubs and there are a couple of independent coffee shops (p20) nearby. Yaletown offers lounge joints for the yuppie set, while the West End houses the city's gay bars.

BC'S BEST BEERS
Vancouver is a great spot to sup British Columbia's best microbrews. On your travels, keep your taste buds peeled for these regional beer-makers and their recommended tipples:
> Granville Island Brewing (Brockton IPA)
> Central City Brewing (Red Racer Classic Pale Ale)
> Storm Brewing (Black Plague Stout)
> Phillips Brewing (Amnesiac IPA)
> Red Truck Beer (Red Truck Lager)
> Crannog Ales (Back Hand of God Stout)
> Howe Sound Brewing (Honey Pale Ale)

🍸 AFTERGLOW *Bar*
☎ 604-602-0835; www.glowbalgrill.com; 1082 Hamilton St; Ⓜ Yaletown-Roundhouse
Tucked at the back of the Glowbal (p47), this intimate room attracts hipsters and Yaletown yuppies in equal measure. Pull-up a block stool and start experimenting with flirty cocktails and ultrastrong bottled Quebec beer. Tapas are also available from the Glowbal menu at this perfect rainy-night cave.

🍸 DIX BBQ & BREWERY *Pub*
☎ 604-682-2739; www.markjamesgroup.com; 871 Beatty St; ⏰ 11:30am-midnight Mon-Fri, 3pm-midnight Sat, 4pm-midnight Sun; Ⓜ Stadium

Popular with hockey and football fans watching big-screen broadcasts, this laid-back brewpub serves some regional BC beers (Red Truck Ale is recommended) as well as its good-value own-brewed tipples. The southern-style nosh rises above regular pub grease-fests – the hearty sausage, shrimp and chicken jambalaya should lure you from the booze.

⛨ FOUNTAINHEAD PUB *Pub*
☎ 604-687-2222; www.thefountain headpub.com; 1025 Davie St; ◷ 11am-midnight Mon-Thu & Sun, 11am-2am Fri & Sat; 🚍 6

On summer evenings, the West End's favorite 'gayborhood' pub is all about the patio, where ogling passing locals and wolf-whistling hand-holding couples parading past is de rigueur. Opt for a quieter evening by heading inside for pub-grub classics or a game of darts with the regulars. If you fancy a pub crawl, the **PumpJack Pub** (☎ 604-685-3417; www.pumpjackpub.com; 1167 Davie St; ◷ 1pm-1am Mon-Thu, 1pm-2am Fri & Sat; 🚍 6) and the loungey **1181** (☎ 604-687-3991; www.tightlounge .com; 1181 Davie St; 🚍 6) are short strolls away. See p53 for clubbing options.

⛨ LENNOX PUB *Pub*
☎ 604-408-0881; 800 Granville St; ◷ 11:30am-11pm Sun-Thu, 11:30am-1am Fri & Sat; Ⓜ Vancouver City Centre

This slender Granville Strip hostelry never has enough tables at weekends, when noise levels prevent all but the most rudimentary of conversations. It's a different story during the week, when calm is restored and you can savor the Sleeman's beers plus a couple of good Belgian drafts. A handy meeting spot for area clubs.

⛨ MARIO'S *Coffee Shop*
☎ 604-608-2804; 595 Howe St; ◷ 6:30am-4:30pm Mon-Fri; 🚍 Burrard

The business district's closely guarded coffee secret, the rich java here is served by Mario himself – he's the fella hovering around his coffee machine as if he's afraid you might swipe it. Expect to be impressed enough to almost forgive the dodgy Italian pop music warbling from the speakers.

⛨ MELRICHE'S *Coffee Shop*
☎ 604-689-5282; 1244 Davie St; ◷ 8am-5pm Mon-Sat, 10am-5pm Sun; ♿ ; 🚍 6

Mismatched wooden tables, hearty cakes and journal-writing locals make this is an ideal rainy-day hangout. Clutch a pail-sized hot chocolate and press your face to the condensation-soaked window: it's the kind of place Morrissey might enjoy on a wet Monday afternoon (although probably not).

MILL MARINE BISTRO *Pub*
☎ 604-687-6455; www.millbistro
.ca; 1199 W Cordova St; ⏲ 11am-11pm
Sun-Wed, 11am-midnight Fri & Sat;
♿ ; Ⓜ **Waterfront**
With mesmerizing views of Burrard Inlet and the North Shore peaks, this seawall bar is all about the patio – arrive early in the evening to ensure you get a table. There's a small but impressive beer selection (Whistler Export Lager is recommended) and you can park the kids at the adjoining free **water park** while you sip away. Also close by is the **Coal Harbour seawalk**.

O'DOUL'S *Bar*
☎ 604-661-1400; www.odoulsrestau
rant.com; 1300 Robson St; ⏲ 11:30am-
midnight; 🚌 5
Downtown's best live-jazz bar and restaurant offers an impressive array of old- and new-world wines, while its beer – served in chilled glasses – includes Granville Island Brewing offerings (ask for the new Brockton IPA). Nightly 9pm performances are free but consider dropping by during the Jazz Festival (p25), when visiting musicians come to jam.

YALETOWN BREWING COMPANY *Pub*
☎ 604-681-2739; 1111 Mainland
St; ⏲ 11:30am-midnight Sun-Wed, 11:30am-1am Thu, 11am-2pm Fri & Sat;
Ⓜ Yaletown-Roundhouse
A chatty, brick-lined bar on one side (including pool tables) and a large restaurant area on the other, both serve the brewery's own-made beers. In summer, the patio is a sought-after perch for ogling Yaletown's beautiful people, but don't drink too much or your chat-up lines will show. For nosh, pizzas are recommended.

⭐ PLAY

Downtown's Granville Strip is Vancouver's mainstream nightlife center, where you'll be jostling with drunken weekend clubbers. Several live-music venues of the indie variety also dot the city center, while gay nightclubs serve locals in the West End. Theater and art-house cinemas also add to the mix.

BC LIONS & BC PLACE STADIUM *Sports Venue*
☎ 604-589-7627; www.bclions.com; BC
Place Stadium; tickets $28-75; ⏲ Jun-
Oct; ♿ ; Ⓜ **Stadium**
The Lions, Vancouver's Canadian Football League (CFL) side, strut their stuff at downtown's cavernous BC Place Stadium. Tickets are generally easy to come by – unless they're closing in on the Grey Cup, when the scalpers will be out in force. Expect a family atmosphere here and a much better ticket

WORTH THE TRIP

From the western end of Water St, the red-brick Waterfront train station (Map pp40–1, F3) looms above you. Now a SkyTrain stop, it's also the departure point for SeaBus (p162) services to North Vancouver. Take the boat – the 12-minute journey itself is worth it – then hop on a No 236 bus to the region's top visitor attraction. The 140m cabled walkway at **Capilano Suspension Bridge & Park** (☎ 604-985-7474; www.capbridge.com; 3735 Capilano Rd; adult/youth/child $27.95/16.65/8.75; ⏱ 8:30am-8pm mid-May–Aug; earlier closing Sep–mid-May; ♿) sways 70m over the fast-running waters of tree-lined Capilano Canyon. It's an awesome sight, especially when you're halfway across and your legs have turned to jelly. The park also has totem poles, historic displays, a network of canopy bridges, Vancouver's biggest souvenir shop and a series of easy rainforest trails – the Cliffhanger Boardwalk, which winds towards the shoreline, is best. Although the bridge continually moves, the span is much more secure than it feels. The original hemp ropes have been replaced with steel cables and 13-ton concrete anchor blocks. The blocks have the same pull as four elephants holding onto each side of the bridge – which would be an even more entertaining attraction.

price than for Canucks hockey games. For more details on the stadium, see p39.

⭐ CAPRICE Nightclub
☎ 604-681-2114; www.capricenight club.com; 967 Granville St; ⏱ 9pm-3am Wed-Sat; 🚌 5
Originally a movie theater, the Caprice is one of the best main-stream haunts on the Granville Strip. The cavernous two-level venue is a thumping magnet for the younger set – expect to have to line up to get in on weekends, when the under-25s dominate. The adjoining lounge is great if you need to rest your eardrums and grab a restorative beer. Sadly, the nearby Plaza has closed its doors.

⭐ COMMODORE Live Music
☎ 604-739-4550; www.livenation.com; 868 Granville St; shows $20-35; 🚌 5
Vancouver's best live-music venue, this old art deco upstairs ballroom has been fully refurbished in recent years but still retains its stepped perimeter tables, mirrored sidebars and that legendary bouncy dance floor that adds extra oomph to mosh-pit shenanigans. Avoid the plastic cups of beer and go for bot-tled Stella Artois.

⭐ MEDIA CLUB Live Music
☎ 604-608-2871; www.themediaclub.ca; 695 Cambie St; shows $5-25; Ⓜ Stadium
Tucked along a backstreet, this low-ceilinged little joint couldn't look less enticing from the outside if it tried. But it's one of the city's

THE 'OTHER' SPORTS TEAM...

The city's other professional sports side is the **Vancouver Whitecaps** (☎ 604-669-9283; www.whitecapsfc.com; Swangard Stadium, Burnaby; tickets $18-35; ☯ Apr-Sep; Ⓜ Patterson; 🚼), a soccer team currently playing its Western Conference League games at Burnaby's draughty old Swangard Stadium, which is about 12km southeast of downtown. Change is coming, though. The team was recently promoted and will begin playing top-level Major League Soccer (MLS) games at downtown's covered BC Place Stadium from 2011. Plans are also being hatched to build a dedicated stadium somewhere in the city center over the next few years. If you want to say you saw them when they were still in Burnaby, wrap up warm – Swangard games can be bloody freezing.

best small music venues, especially if you like your indie bands to be a bit more rocking than the usual wimpy singer-songwriters. Check ahead to see what's on and consider bringing earplugs.

🌟 ODYSSEY *Nightclub*
☎ 604-689-5256; www.theodyssey nightclub.com; 1251 Howe St; ☯ from 9pm nightly; 🚌 10

The city's leading gay nightclub offers a predictably hot and heavy roster of nightly events that leads up to the weekend's loud and throbbing Friday and Saturday dance nights – caged men and whipping cream provided. The club was considering moving at time of research, so check ahead before slipping into your drag outfit. The city's other main gay club is Davie St's **Celebrities** (☎ 604-681-6180; www.ce lebritiesnightclub.com; 1022 Davie St; ☯ from 9pm Tue-Sat; 🚌 6), an equally pumping venue, especially on Saturdays.

🌟 RAILWAY CLUB *Live Music*
☎ 604-681-1625; www.therailway club.com; 579 Dunsmuir St; free-$10; Ⓜ Granville

The fabulous little 'Rail' combines a comfortably worn, Brit-style bar and a tiny stage showcasing nightly acts ranging from indie to folk and beat poetry. Arrive before 7pm – the easy-to-miss doorway is next to the 7-11 and the venue is up some stairs – to avoid cover charges. Spend your savings on BC microbrews from Phillips and Central City.

🌟 SPOKES BICYCLE RENTAL
Activity
☎ 604-688-5141; www.spokesbicycle rentals.com; 1798 W Georgia St; per hr/6 hr from $9.50/28; ☯ 9am-7pm May-Aug, 10am-dusk Sep-Apr; 🚼 ; 🚌 19

Located near Stanley Park's W Georgia St entrance, this is the cycle-rental shop of choice for those who want to trundle around the seawall but forgot to pack their bike. Expect to take an hour or two to traverse the entire 8.8km loop and try to not to take out any tourists that may be wandering in your path.

⭐ VANCITY THEATRE *Cinema*
☎ 604-683-3456; www.viff.org; 1181 Seymour St; admission $10; 🚍 10
Headquarters of the Film Festival (p27), this state-of-the-art cinema offers new-run documentaries, foreign movies and specialty showings, along with visiting mini festivals and lectures. It's a similar story at the older **Pacific Cinémathèque** (☎ 604-688-3456; www.cinematheque.bc.ca; 1131 Howe St; admission $9.50; 🚍 10), where classic kid matinees and horror and film noir festivals add to the mix.

⭐ VANCOUVER CANUCKS (GM PLACE STADIUM) *Sports Venue*
☎ 604-899-4600; www.canucks.com; GM Place; $55-131; 🕙 Oct-Apr; Ⓜ Stadium
The NHL's Canucks are a religion to ice-hockey-loving Vancouverites – which means packed sports bars on game nights, city-wide street celebrations if the Stanley Cup play-offs progress and sold-to-capacity games at GM Place. If you can't snag a ticket, catch the good-value Western Hockey League's **Vancouver Giants** (☎ 604-444-2687; www.vancouvergiants.com; Pacific Coliseum; $16.50-

18.50; 🕙 Sep-Mar; 🚍 10) at the Pacific Coliseum instead, which is about 1.5km east of Commercial Dr.

⭐ VANCOUVER PLAYHOUSE
Theater
☎ 604-873-3311; www.vancouverplayhouse.com; cnr Hamilton & Dunsmuir Sts; tickets $33-66; Ⓜ Stadium
Formerly little more than a humdrum provincial theater, the city's top dramatic troupe has upped its game in recent years, delivering seasons that mix eye-opening reinterpretations of contemporary classics with occasional new plays that shake the floorboards. The six-play season runs from October to around April.

⭐ VANCOUVER SYMPHONY ORCHESTRA/ORPHEUM THEATRE *Live Music*
☎ 604-876-3434; www.vancouversymphony.ca; locations vary; tickets $25-60; 🚍 5
Offering accessible classics and 'pops,' the beloved VSO usually performs at downtown's atmospheric old Orpheum Theatre, the city's favorite heritage auditorium on 884 Granville St. Aside from visiting soloist concerts and Sunday matinees, special shows include Kid Koncerts and film nights, when live scores are performed to classic flicks. If enamored of the Orpheum, take a summer backstage tour (p166).

>STANLEY PARK

Named after the fella who also gave his moniker to the Stanley Cup ice-hockey trophy, this spectacular 400-hectare green space is the city's outdoorsy jewel – as well as North America's largest urban park (eat your heart out New York). Bristling with an estimated half-million fir, cedar and hemlock trees, the nature-hugging waterfront peninsula was originally settled by First Nations villagers before becoming a public park during the colonial era – some indigenous residents were still living here when it opened in 1888.

Since then, it's become a sigh-triggering playground for locals and visitors who walk, jog, cycle or rollerblade the picture-perfect seawall and hit attractions including the aquarium, swimming pool and the brightly colored totem poles. Of course, you don't have to be busy to enjoy yourself here: bring a picnic, find a grassy promontory and be sure to catch a languid sunset from Third Beach.

STANLEY PARK

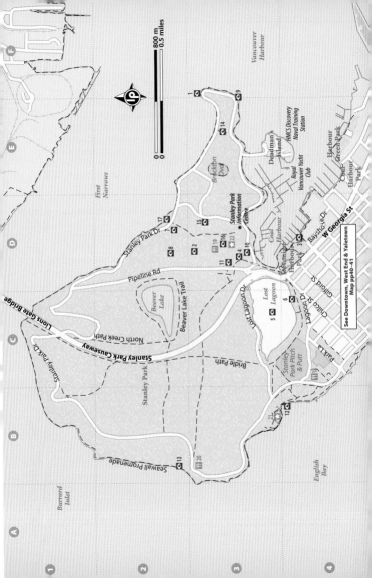

👁 SEE

It's not just about the 8.8km seawall here – see p11 for a summary of the park – although you'd be nuts not to wander along at least part of it to catch a few breathtaking mountain-backed waterfront vistas. Once you've drained your camera battery, check the park's interior for tree-shaded trails, great kid-friendly attractions and a smattering of surprises.

👁 BROCKTON POINT

This leg-shaped promontory, a short seawall stroll from the W Georgia St entrance, is the first stop for many visitors. They come for the eight brightly colored **totem poles** and three beautifully carved Coast Salish welcome portals that recall the park's original residents. Nearby is a bronze statue of sprinter Harry Jerome, who, as a six-time world record holder, was British Columbia's athlete of the last century. Skirting the seafront, you'll also find the **Nine O'Clock Gun** that booms at 9pm every night.

👁 HARBOR CRUISES

☎ 604-688-7246; www.boatcruises.com; north foot of Denman St; adult/youth/child $30/25/10; ⏱ Apr–early Oct; 🚌 19

A lone jogger heads into the distance along the seawall at Stanely Park (p56)

STANLEY PARK'S HIDDEN STATUES

Vancouver's favorite playground is teeming with statues and memorials, many of them now hidden or forgotten. Start your treasure hunt with the statue of Lord Frederic Arthur Stanley himself, who nestles in the trees with his arms outstretched to welcome visitors. A short stroll away is the fragrant rose garden. Also close by stands a larger figure, this one depicting Scottish wordsmith Robert Burns, which was unveiled in 1928 by UK Prime Minister Ramsay MacDonald. At the back of the Malkin Bowl seating area, there's an often overlooked memorial to Warren Harding, marking the first official visit to Canada by a US president. It's a memorial because he died a week later in San Francisco.

View the city skyline and some unexpected wildlife from the water on a 75-minute harbor tour, departing close to Stanley Park's W Georgia St entrance. The replica paddle steamer is the most fun way to go and you'll hear a few stories about the park along the way. Lunch and dinner cruises are also offered (think salmon buffet), as well as a tranquil excursion to Indian Arm.

◎ LOST LAGOON

If you're sick of the tour-bus crowds, take a restorative loop around this expansive, tree-backed pond, keeping your eyes peeled for a blue heron or two standing stock-still just off the shoreline. The friendly folk at the **Lost Lagoon Nature House** (☎ 604-257-8544; www.stanleyparkecology.ca; admission free; ☷ 10am-7pm Tue-Sun May-Sep; ♿) on the southern shore can fill you in on the park's ecosystem and the staff also offer regular guided nature walks. To the west is family-

friendly **Second Beach**, which also boasts an outdoor swimming pool (see p63) and is a place where you can pick up an ice cream.

◎ MINIATURE RAILWAY & CHILDREN'S FARMYARD

☎ 604-257-8531; railway adult/youth/child $6/4.25/3; ☷ 10:30am-5pm mid-May–Aug, 10:30am-5pm Sat & Sun Feb–mid-May & Sep, plus special Halloween and Christmas services; farmyard adult/youth/child $6/4.25/3; ☷ 11am-4pm mid-May–Aug, 11am-4pm Sat & Sun Feb–mid-May & Sep; ♿ ; ☐ 19 Twin, kid-friendly attractions overrun with giddy youngsters in summer, the farmyard is all about hanging out with smelly llamas, sheep, goats, cows and pettable rabbits. The adjacent railway is a 15-minute train trundle through the forest that's transformed into a fairy-light covered spook fest for Halloween and a fantastic Yuletide wonderland at Christmas. Aqua fans should also partake of the free, giggle-triggering **water park** on the seawall near Lumberman's Arch.

VANCOUVER AQUARIUM

☎ 604-659-3474; www.vanaqua.org; adult/youth/child $20/15/12; ⏲ 9:30am-5pm Sep-Jun, 9:30am-7pm Jul & Aug; ♿ ; 🚌 19

Home to sharks, dolphins and a clutch of beluga whales, the aquarium is one of Vancouver's biggest attractions, so arrive early on peak summer days. Check out the mesmerizing iridescent jellyfish tanks, the sea otters that eat swimming on their backs (try it at home) and the lazy sloth that moves so infrequently it might actually be stuffed. Behind-the-scenes **tours** (adult/child from $25/15) are recommended.

🍴 EAT

If you haven't brought a picnic, you won't go hungry here and, if you overindulge you can sprint around the seawall a few times. Reward your exercise with a concession-stand ice cream.

Beluga whales delight the visitors to the Vancouver Aquarium (above)

WORTH THE TRIP

If you're driving to Stanley Park, continue along the causeway, cross Lions Gate Bridge and you'll soon be on the North Shore, comprising North Vancouver and West Vancouver. You could drive up to Capilano Suspension Bridge (p53) or you could partake of the three outdoorsy hot spots that lie on Vancouver's doorstep. **Grouse Mountain** (☎ 604-980-9311; www.grousemountain.com; 6400 Nancy Greene Way; SkyRide admission adult/youth/child $34.95/20.95/12.95, winter ski lift adult/youth/child $52.50/42/23.10; ☼ 9am-10pm; 🏃 ; 🚌 236 from the SeaBus Lonsdale Quay) touts itself as the 'peak of Vancouver.' In summer, your SkyRide ticket gives you mountain-top access to restaurants, hiking trails, a cheeky lumberjack show and a grizzly bear refuge where two inhabitants lumber around just a few feet from the cameras. A zipline course was also recently installed and an elevator-accessed viewing platform was being added on our visit.

If you don't want to pay for entry, you can join the throng hiking up the steep and unforgiving 2.9km Grouse Grind trail. Bring water, expect to suffer and don't give up. It's a one-way trail, but grinders can buy a special $5 ticket to take the SkyRide down. In winter, Grouse is Vancouver's favorite snow-covered playground, with 26 ski and snowboard runs, marked snowshoe trails, a small ice rink and plenty of après-ski shenanigans.

A less busy nature escape from the city and a great spot to hug 500-year-old Douglas firs, **Mt Seymour Provincial Park** (☎ 604-986-9371; www.bcparks.ca; 1700 Mt Seymour Rd) is crisscrossed with hiking and mountain-biking trails. Some areas are rugged, so backpackers should register at the park office, where trail maps are also available. Like Grouse, the park transforms in winter, when **Mt Seymour Resorts** (☎ 604-986-2261; www.mountseymour.com; adult/youth/child $42/35/21; ☼ 9:30am-10pm Mon-Fri, 8:30am-10pm Sat & Sun Jan-Mar; 🏃) runs five lifts to take you skiing or snowboarding on its 23 runs. There are also 10km of snowshoe trails, an eight-run toboggan area and a four-lane tubing course. To get to Seymour, take the Mt Seymour Parkway exit east, then turn north on Mt Seymour Rd. Alternatively, **Cypress Coach Lines** (☎ 604-637-7669; www.cypresscoachlines.com; return $20) operates a winter shuttle to the mountain from points around Vancouver.

Nestled in the mountains 8km north of West Van, **Cypress Provincial Park** (☎ 604-924-2200; www.bcparks.ca) has great summertime hiking trails and a cool bike park. In winter, its **Cypress Mountain** (☎ 604-926-5612; www.cypressmountain.com; adult/youth/child $60/49.50/29.50; ☼ 9am-10pm mid-Dec–Mar, 9am-4pm Mar–season end; 🏃 ; 🚌 shuttle departs Parkgate Mall winter, $5) ski area competes for local powder nuts with six lifts, 52 runs and superior average snowfall – plus some snowshoeing, tubing and cross-country skiing courses. Since being chosen as the freestyle-skiing and snowboarding venue for the 2010 Olympics (p123), facilities at Cypress have been given a long-overdue upgrade (including the swanky new Cypress Creek Lodge). If you're driving, follow the highway through Stanley Park, take Exit 8 and then follow the signs along Cypress Bowl Rd.

NEIGHBORHOODS

STANLEY PARK

FISH HOUSE IN STANLEY PARK *Seafood* $$$

☎ 604-681-7275; www.fishhouse stanleypark.com; 8901 Stanley Park Dr; mains $14-30; ⏱ 11:30am-10pm Mon-Sat, 11am-10pm Sun; 🚌 19

The park's fine-dining superstar, this swanky eatery serves some of the city's best seafood treats. The top-end menu changes season-ally but regular favorites include cedar-planked trout and chili sablefish – there's also a popular fresh oyster bar that lures in-the-know shuckers. Weekend brunch is a menu highlight and the salmon bagel Benedict is highly recommended.

STANLEY'S PARK BAR & GRILL *Comfort Food* $$

☎ 604-602-3088; www.stanleysbar .ca; 610 Pipeline Rd; mains $11-19; ⏱ 11:30am-10pm Jun-Sep; 🚌 19

Overlooking landscaped gardens and the Malkin Bowl theater, this laid-back resto-bar combo has the park's biggest patio. The interior is

The dining room of the Teahouse restaurant (opposite) looks over English Bay

all about slate floors and chunky polished wood counters, while the menu is a smorgasbord of high-end comfort food such as prime rib burgers and salmon ciabattas. Equally good for an end-of-day beer, the bar's microbrews include local Red Truck Lager.

TEAHOUSE *West Coast* $$
☎ 604-669-3281, 800-280-9493; Ferguson Point; mains $16-35; ⏱ noon-10pm; 🚌 19

Formerly the old Teahouse, then Sequoia Grill and now resurrected as the new Teahouse, this cheery-chic spot combines a brightly painted, artsy interior with a small menu of seasonal classics, often including Cornish hen, pan-seared venison or maple-marinated wild salmon. Delivering well-executed contemporary nosh, it beats rivals across the city with some killer ocean views. Nearby **Third Beach** is arguably the best spot in Vancouver to find a nice spot from which to view the sunset.

PLAY

MALKIN BOWL *Theater*
☎ 604-734-1917; www.tuts.ca; tickets $29-36; ⏱ mid-Jul–Aug; 🚌 19

Built in 1934, this evocative alfresco auditorium comes alive every summer when Theatre Under the Stars stages two crowd-pleasing good-time musicals. Recent years have also seen a few bands (including the Raconteurs and the New Pornographers) treading the creaky boards with a concert or two.

SECOND BEACH POOL
Activity
☎ 604-257-8370; www.vancouverparks.ca; cnr N Lagoon Dr & Stanley Park Dr; adult/youth/child $5.15/3.60/2.60; ⏱ May-Sep; 🏊 🚼 ; 🚌 19

A magnet for fun-loving families throughout the summer season, this jewel-like outdoor pool enjoys a spectacular waterfront setting. You'll have to arrive early to stake out your spot but your kids will thank you for dragging them from their beds.

>GASTOWN & CHINATOWN

Named after 'Gassy' Jack Deighton, a chatty Yorkshireman who rowed in with a whiskey barrel in the 1860s and started a bar that triggered a small settlement, Gastown was the forerunner of modern-day Vancouver. But the cobbled area entered a skid-row decline during the last century, only to be rescued and renovated by history-hugging locals since the 1970s. The reclamation has taken a long time and only in recent years has Gastown become a welcoming area of characterful bars and indie stores.

Historic appeal is also a major part of the charm in the adjoining Chinatown district, one of the largest in North America. Colored with flare-roofed heritage buildings and animated with bustling stores and businesses, it's the ideal spot for a half-day wander. Both areas overlap with the worst sections of the intriguing but fairly dodgy Downtown Eastside (see p68), where street smarts are recommended.

GASTOWN & CHINATOWN

🔘 SEE
Dominion Building 1 A3
Dr Sun Yat-Sen Classical
   Chinese Garden 2 B4
Flack Block 3 A3
Gassy Jack Statue ....(see 4)
Maple Tree Square 4 B3
Millennium Gate 5 B4
Omnimax Theatre ....(see 6)
Science World at Telus World
   of Science 6 B6
Steam Clock 7 A2
Vancouver Police Centennial
   Museum 8 C3
Woodward's Building 9 A3

🛍 SHOP
Chinatown Night
   Market 10 C4
John Fluevog Shoes 11 B2
Wanted - Lost Found
   Canadian 12 C3

🍴 EAT
Deacon's Corner 13 C2
Hon's Wun-Tun House ...14 C4
Irish Heather 15 B3
La Casita 16 B3
New Town Bakery &
   Restaurant 17 C4
Salt Tasting Room 18 B3

🍸 DRINK
Alibi Room 19 C2
Boneta 20 B3
Six Acres 21 B3
Steamworks Brewing
   Co 22 A2

⭐ PLAY
Cobalt 23 C5
Firehall Arts Centre 24 C3
Modern 25 B2
Shine 26 A2

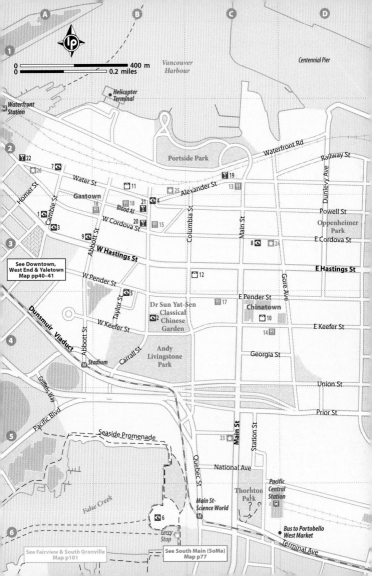

Gastown, Chinatown & East Vancouver

A **B** **C** **D**

1

Vancouver Harbour

Centennial Pier

0 ——————— 400 m
0 ——————— 0.2 miles

Waterfront
Station

Helicopter
Terminal

2

☕22

🍴26   7 🕐

Water St

Portside Park

Waterfront Rd

Railway St

Dunlevy Ave

🍴11

🍴25 Alexander St   13 🍴

19 🍴

Gastown

🏛18 21 🍴

Blood Al

4 🍴

Powell St

1 🏛   Cambie St

🏛3

W Cordova St

20 🍴   15 🍴

Columbia St

Main St

Oppenheimer
Park

E Cordova St

Homer St

3

9 🍴

Abbott St

W Hastings St

8 🕐   24 ★

E Hastings St

See Downtown,
West End & Yaletown
Map pp40–41

W Pender St

12 🏛

Gore Ave

Dunsmuir Viaduct

5 🍴

Taylor St

E Pender St

17 🍴

Chinatown

🏛10

4

Carrall St

W Keefer St

*Dr Sun Yat-Sen
Classical
Chinese
Garden*

🏛2

E Keefer St

14 🍴

Stadium

*Andy
Livingstone
Park*

Georgia St

Griffiths Way

Union St

5

Pacific Blvd

Seaside Promenade

Main St

23 🍴

Station St

Prior St

False Creek

Quebec St

National Ave

*Pacific
Central
Station*

*Thorn ton
Park*

6

6 🍴

Ferry
Stop

*Main St-
Science World*

Bus to Portobello
West Market

See Fairview & South Granville
Map p101

See South Main (SoMa)
Map p77

Terminal Ave

GASTOWN & CHINATOWN

👁 SEE

The 'Gassy' Jack Deighton's statue on Maple Tree Sq marks the hub of Gastown. Going south, start your Chinatown meander at the towering **Millennium Gate** (cnr Pender & Taylor Sts) then stroll eastward to the heart of the matter.

👁 DR SUN YAT-SEN CLASSICAL CHINESE GARDEN & PARK

☎ 604-662-3207; www.vancouver chinesegarden.com; 578 Carrall St; garden adult/child $10/8; admission park free; 🕙 10am-6pm May–mid-Jun & Sep, 9.30am-7pm mid-Jun–Aug, 10am-4:30pm Oct-Apr; Ⓜ Stadium

This Taoist-inspired landscaped garden includes pagoda-topped walkways, oddly shaped limestone lumps and gnarly fingered pine trees, all encircling a jade-colored pond rippling with laconic turtles. The fascinating 45-minute tour shows you how to tell your yin from your yang and there are also alfresco concerts here on select summer evenings. The similar but less grand park next door is free.

👁 SCIENCE WORLD AT TELUS WORLD OF SCIENCE

☎ 604-443-7440; www.scienceworld .ca; 1455 Quebec St; adult/youth/child $18.75/15.25/12.75; 🕙 10am-5pm Mon-Fri, 10am-6pm Sat & Sun; 👶 ; Ⓜ Main St-Science World 🚢 Science World

Unleash your inner child (or just elbow aside the real under-10s) at the city's family-friendly geodesic dome landmark. You'll find two levels of hands-on science, technology and nature exhibits, including a gallery exploring sustainability, and a watercourse with ball cannons and bridges. On top of Science World, the large-format **Omnimax Theatre** (tickets $10) screens eye-popping documentary movies.

STEAM CLOCK SHOCK

Halfway along Water St, you'll suddenly find yourself battling crowds of camera-wielding tourists hanging around an otherwise inauspicious street corner. Look up and you'll see the object of their giddy attention. Symbolizing Gastown's 1970s restoration drive, this kitsch clock-tower landmark was apparently modeled on Big Ben (presumably by someone who'd never actually seen the real thing). The clock is famous for marking 15-minute increments with toots from its steam whistles, but the mechanism is actually driven by electricity (this is a dark and dastardly secret that tourists are never supposed to find out). The whistles – the top one was salvaged from the *SS Beaver*, which ran aground near Stanley Park in 1888 – are powered from an underground steam heat system that also serves local buildings.

◉ VANCOUVER POLICE CENTENNIAL MUSEUM

☎ 604-665-3346; www.vancouverpolice museum.ca; 240 E Cordova St; adult/child $7/5; 🕙 9am-5pm Mon-Sat; 🚌 7

Contextualizing the history of crime-and-vice-addled Downtown Eastside streets surrounding it, this quirky museum is lined with confiscated weapons, counterfeit currency and a grizzly former mortuary room where the walls are studded with preserved slivers of human tissue – spot the bullet-damaged brain slices. Ask about the excellent summertime Sins of the City area walking tour.

Dr Sun Yat-Sen Classical Chinese Garden (opposite)

🛍 SHOP

Chinatown is a visual feast of old-style apothecaries, tea shops and grocery stores where unfamiliar produce (anyone for lizard splayed on a stick?) spills across the sidewalks. Gastown's old stone-built piles are colonized with some of Vancouver's best indie stores – check along Water St plus the short stretch of W Cordova St between Water and Cambie Sts.

🛍 CHINATOWN NIGHT MARKET *Market*

☎ 604-682-8998; 100-200 Keefer St; 🕙 6:30-11pm Fri-Sun mid-May–mid-Sep; 🚌 8

Squint a little and you could almost be in Hong Kong at this small but colorful nighttime bazaar that lures with its cheap trinkets, dodgy DVDs and walk-through smorgasbord of steaming noodles, fish balls and bubble tea. There's live music on most nights and if you haven't stuffed yourself at the stalls, there are lots of surrounding restaurants calling your name for dinner.

🛍 JOHN FLUEVOG SHOES *Shoes*

☎ 604-688-6228; www.fluevog.com; 65 Water St; 🕙 11am-7pm Mon-Wed, 11am-8pm Thu & Fri, 11am-7pm Sat, noon-6pm Sun; 🚌 8

Real Vancouverites own at least one pair of shoes from this local

TRAWL THE CITY'S FORGOTTEN NEIGHBORHOOD

Vancouver's one-time commercial heartland, the Downtown Eastside has become a ghetto of lives wasted by drugs and prostitution in recent years. But, triggered by the massive new Woodward's redevelopment, the neighborhood that time forgot is rising, encouraging visitors with street smarts to check it out. The area radiates from E Hastings St, primarily between Cambie and Main Sts.

What you'll find is a clutch of paint-peeled historic buildings that survived the era when similar structures in other neighborhoods were demolished. Ripe for renovation, many are finally being reclaimed. Check out the preserved **Dominion Building** (Map p65; 205 W Hastings St) for an idea of the structures that once defined the area, then stroll east past the newly restored **Flack Block** (Map p65; 163 W Hastings St) and next door's **Woodward's** (Map p65; 105 W Hastings St), now home to retail, housing and a college campus.

Continue from here (avoiding the back alleys) for heritage neon signs such as Save-on-Meats and Only Seafoods Café, then nip into **Wanted - Lost Found Canadian** (below), one of the area's revitalizing shops.

Next, walk to the corner of Hastings and Main Sts, the eye-opening center of the area's troubled population. It provides a PR-free alternative to Vancouver's 'world's best city' claims. From here, stroll to the **Vancouver Police Centennial Museum** (p67) for some crime-fighting context on the area.

footwear legend, now firmly established in this cavernous flagship store. Pick up that pair of thigh-hugging dominatrix boots you've always wanted or settle on some designer-twisted brogues that look exactly like Doc Martens on acid.

☐ WANTED – LOST FOUND CANADIAN *Homewares*
☎ 604-633-0178; 436 Columbia St;
⌚ noon-5pm Mon-Sat; 🚍 8
Hidden in a former barbershop along a grubby Downtown Eastside side street, this artsy little business recycles old blankets, beach glass, gnarled driftwood

and whatever else the owners can find into new patchwork bags, fluffy cushions and eclectic accessories – even dusty newspapers discovered under the floorboards are now unique greeting cards.

🍴 EAT

Chinatown – especially on Pender St – is replete with great noshing options. Adjoining Gastown offers infinitely more variety, with mainstream joints on Water St and, if you hunt along the side streets, some West Coast and international-inspired eateries. Don't forget Gastown's bars either as they offer some of Vancouver's best comfort-food dining.

🍴 BONETA *International* $$

☎ 604-684-1844; www.boneta.ca; 1 W Cordova St; mains $14-26; ⏲ noon-4pm & 5:30pm-midnight Mon-Sat, noon-midnight Sun; 🚌 8

Typifying Gastown's transformation, this old bank building now houses a bold eatery where the chef's imagination is sparked by seasonal regional ingredients. Expect taste-tripping riffs such as smoked bison carpaccio with sherry vinaigrette or grilled rack of lamb with curried cauliflower.

There's a small but excellent wine selection, but start with a cocktail or two, the bar's specialty.

🍴 DEACON'S CORNER
Comfort Food $

☎ 604-684-1555; www.deaconscorner .ca; 101 Main St; mains $6-13; ⏲ 7am-3pm Mon-Fri, 10am-3pm Sat & Sun; 🚌 8

The perfect Gastown combination of new gentrification and old-school good value, since its 2009 opening this mod neighborhood diner has been luring Vancouverites to a grubby part of town they've previously avoided. Esurient locals come for the heaping,

Having a snack at legendary Hon's Wun-Tun House (p70) in Chinatown

GASTOWN & CHINATOWN

hangover-busting breakfasts (the Hungry Man is recommended if you haven't eaten for a month) plus hearty lunchtime fare such as Reuben sandwiches and the excellent Cobb salad.

🍴 HON'S WUN-TUN HOUSE
Chinese $$
☎ 604-688-0871; www.hons.ca; 268 E Keefer St; dishes $6-18; 🕙 11am-11pm Sun-Thu, 11am-midnight Sat & Sun; 🚌 8
The 300-plus menu options at this clamorous Chinatown legend range from satisfying dim-sum brunches to steaming wun-tun soups bobbling with juicy dumplings. For something different, try the good-value congee rice porridge – a fancy-free dish that takes three hours to prepare and comes in seafood, chicken and beef varieties: it'll lag your stomach for a day's worth of walking.

🍴 IRISH HEATHER
Gastropub $$
☎ 604-688-9779; www.irishheather .com; 212 Carrall St; mains $15-17; 🕙 noon-midnight; 🚌 8
A wood-lined boozer on one side (with a floor made from old Guinness barrels) and a giant communal table space on the other, this is Vancouver's best gastropub. You'll find perfectly poured stout, a diverse array of alternative tipples (try Saskatoon's Black Cat

Lager) and a menu of deep steak pies, house-cured charcuterie plates and tapas (try the crisp-fried cauliflower with hummus).

🍴 LA CASITA *Mexican* $$
☎ 604-646-2444; www.lacasita.ca; 101 W Cordova St; mains $8-16; 🕙 11:30am-10pm Mon & Tue, 11:30am-11pm Wed & Thu, 11:30am-midnight Fri & Sat, 2-10pm Sun; 🅥 ; 🚌 8
You'll feel instantly welcome in this cocoon-like family-run Mexican joint, especially with a couple of margarita pitchers and the fairy lights casting their cozy glow. Slow down and settle in for the evening, with some shrimp and salmon tacos, chicken or chorizo chimichangas and a bowl of fortifying black-bean soup. Veggie options abound.

🍴 NEW TOWN BAKERY & RESTAURANT *Chinese* $
☎ 604-662-3300; 158 E Pender St; dishes $5-9; 🕙 6:30am-8.30pm; 🚌 8
Ideal pit stop for a Chinatown wander, this chatty Asian diner specializes in steam buns, Chinese pastries and dim sum, served from giant steamers on the counter. Warm, moist barbecue pork buns are a recommended takeout – there's not much of an ambience here, so there's no real reason to stick around. The buns also come in vegetarian varieties.

SALT TASTING ROOM
Comfort Food $$
☎ 604-633-1912; www.salttastingroom
.com; Blood Alley; plates $5-15; ⏱ noon-
midnight; 🚌 8

Tucked along a cobbled back
alley insalubriously named after
the area's former butcher trade,
this chatty, brick-lined charcuterie
and wine bar is a protein-lover's
delight. Pull up a communal table
stool and peruse the blackboard
offerings of house-cured meats
and regional cheeses, then go
for the $15 tasting plate of three,
served with a dash of Brit-style
piccalilli.

🍸 DRINK

Gastown is Vancouver's best bar
area and you can plan an easy
pub crawl in and around Maple
Tree Sq where Carrall, Water and
Alexander Sts collide. For a sum-
mary of Gastown's bars and pubs,
see p14.

🍸 ALIBI ROOM *Bar*
☎ 604-623-3383; www.alibi.ca; 157
Alexander St; ⏱ 5pm-midnight Tue-Thu,
5am-1pm Fri, 5am-1am Sat, 10am-3pm
Sun; 🚌 8

Completely reinvented as Vancou-
ver's best British Columbia (BC)

Pouring a beer at the Alibi Room (above) in Gastown

Nigel Springthorpe
Co-owner of the Alibi Room, expat Brit and strong supporter of BC microbreweries

How many beers do you serve here? Nineteen mostly BC drafts, three guest casks and 20-plus carefully chosen bottles – mostly Belgian beers that brewers here don't make. **Current favorites** Rasputin Imperial Stout and Red Racer IPA; it competes with the best IPAs in North America. **Best beer for microbrew virgins** Driftwood wheat beer – it's flavored with coriander and orange – and is a great 'entry level' brew. **Most adventurous tipple** Flemish-style Menage a Trois: it's for hardcore beer guys. **Ideal line-your-stomach strategy** The Canadian cheese plate or a bison flatiron steak. **Favorite other Vancouver bars** Six Acres (opposite), Irish Heather (p70) and Cascade Room (p82). **Recommended hangover cure** Biscuits and gravy at Deacon's Corner (p69).

microbrewery bar in recent years, join the chatty communal tables and taste-trip through celebrated regional beers such as Back Hand of God stout and the excellent Old Yale Pale Ale. Check the guest kegs and consider a sample rack of four tipples if you're feeling adventurous. Food is of the gourmet comfort-food variety (duck wrap is recommended).

A tasting plate at the Salt Tasting Room (p71) on Blood Alley in Gastown

SIX ACRES *Bar*

☎ 604-488-0110; www.sixacres.ca; 203 Carrall St; ⏰ 5pm-midnight Tue-Thu, 5pm-1am Fri & Sat; ⃞ 8

Named after the size of the original pre-Vancouver township that started here, this cozy, brick-lined hangout is beloved of Gastown's urban hipsters. There's a small, chatty patio out front but the inside is ideal for hiding in a candlelit corner and working your way through a spectacular array of bottled brews such as Phillips IPA, Propeller Bitter and several piquant Belgian tipples. A menu of shareable tasting plates includes the recommended Olympian. When you head upstairs to the washrooms, expect to be regaled by German-language tapes or the Orson Welles radio recording of *War of the Worlds*.

STEAMWORKS BREWING COMPANY *Bar*

☎ 604-689-2739; www.steamworks .com; 375 Water St; ⏰ 11:30am-midnight Sun-Wed; 11:30am-1am Thu-Sat; Ⓜ Waterfront

This cavernous converted warehouse building makes its own brews on-site, including the signature Lions Gate Lager. Head downstairs for a buzzing pub atmosphere (upstairs is more like a restaurant) and soak up the booze with one of the popular thin-crust pizzas. Drop

NEIGHBORHOODS

GASTOWN & CHINATOWN

CHINATOWN'S FORGOTTEN STREET

Immediately past Chinatown's giant Millennium Gate, Shanghai Alley looks like a quiet backstreet and not the clamor suggested by its name. In fact, this stretch was originally home to hundreds of Chinese immigrant men who arrived to work on the Canadian Pacific Railway in the mid- to late 1800s. The thoroughfare was lined with Chinese shops and businesses at the time and even had its own 500-seat Sing Kew Theatre, the centerpiece of the area's thriving nightlife. Strolling the alley today, you'll find a giant Chinese bell memorial marking the city's rich Asian history.

by for the monthly **Green Drinks** (www.greendrinks.org) event when local eco-huggers roll in to chat.

PLAY

COBALT *Live Music*
☎ 604-764-7865; www.thecobalt.net; 917 Main St; cover free–$10; 🚌 8
Punk, hardcore and metal fans have made the dodgy old Cobalt their fave live venue in recent years. Don't be put off by its grungy location: there's a welcoming crowd of black-clad musos here, while the bands – think Mallhavoc, Fiends and the delightfully named Pissups – are of the blistering, ear-bleeding variety. Not a good spot to read a book.

FIREHALL ARTS CENTRE
Theater
☎ 604-689-0926; www.firehallarts centre.ca; 280 E Cordova St; tickets $10–30; 🚌 10
Leading the city's avant-garde theater scene, this studio-sized venue is housed in an old fire station. Happenings include culturally diverse, contemporary drama and dance, with an emphasis on emerging talent. There's an additional outdoor-courtyard stage and a convivial licensed lounge where visiting thesps and drama fans run chins over a few beers. The season runs from September to June.

MODERN *Nightclub*
☎ 604-647-0121; www.dhmbars.ca; 7 Alexander St; cover $10; Ⓜ Waterfront
Nestled in a Gastown heritage block, this sleek, classy and ultra-contemporary lounge-nightclub combo attracts an over-20s crowd with money to burn on decadent cocktails. That doesn't mean they don't like to dance: Monday is rap night; Friday is electro, dance and rave; while Saturday's clamorous La Discoteque is all about innovative electro and house shenanigans.

SHINE *Nightclub*
☎ 604-408-4321; www.shinenight club.com; 364 Water St; cover $5-10; Ⓜ Waterfront

The dance floor at Shine (opposite) in Gastown

From electro to funky house and hip-hop, Gastown's sexy, subterranean Shine attracts a younger crowd and is divided into a noisy main room and an intimate cozy cave with a long chill-out sofa.

The club's Saturday night 'Big Sexy Funk' (hip-hop and rock) is ever popular but Thursday's retro night appeals to all those elderly 25-year-old hipsters who still remember the '90s.

>SOUTH MAIN (SOMA)

Originally a part of the old working-class Mount Pleasant district, the area was given the 'SoMa' moniker in the 1990s when developers were trying to reclaim the grubby, paint-peeled South Main St strip as a hip new 'hood. The gentrification drive worked and the area is now home to many of Vancouver's leading independent stores, bars and eateries.

For first-timers, the neighborhood is best divided into two: the few blocks around the Main and E Broadway intersection represents the showier end, complete with the kind of character coffee joints where Puma-wearing locals sip espressos behind top-quality Apple laptops. Then there is the area further south, past dry-cleaners and humdrum family diners, around the 20th Ave intersection, where you'll suddenly hit another pocket of cool. This second stretch is studded with eclectic indie shops, serving the bright young things that colonize the wooden heritage homes lining the area's side streets.

SOUTH MAIN (SOMA)

◉ SEE
Bus to Portobello West
    Market 1 C1
Olympic Athletes Village ..2 A1
Portobello West Market 3 D2

🏠 SHOP
Front & Company 4 B5
JEM Gallery 5 B3
Lazy Susan's 6 B5
Mountain Equipment
    Co-op 7 A3
Red Cat Records 8 B6

Regional Assembly of
    Text 9 B5
Smoking Lily 10 B5
Twigg & Hottie 11 B5

🍴 EAT
Argo Café 12 B2
Chutney Villa 13 B3
Foundation 14 B2
Liberty Bakery 15 B5
Slickity Jim's Chat &
    Chew 16 B3
Three Lions Café 17 B3

🍸 DRINK
Cascade Room 18 B3
Gene Café 19 B3
Whip 20 B2

★ PLAY
Biltmore Cabaret 21 C3

See Downtown, West End & Yaletown Map pp40–41

See Gastown & Chinatown Map p65

See Commercial Drive Map p85

See Fairview & South Granville Map p101

Main St–Science World

Rocky Mountaineer Station

Terminal Ave

Industrial Ave

W 1st Ave — E 1st Ave
W 2nd Ave — E 2nd Ave
W 3rd Ave — E 3rd Ave
W 4th Ave — E 4th Ave
W 5th Ave — E 5th Ave
W 6th Ave — E 6th Ave
W 7th Ave — E 7th Ave
Jonathan Rogers Park
W 8th Ave — E 8th Ave
W Broadway — E Broadway
W 10th Ave — E 10th Ave
W 11th Ave — E 11th Ave
W 12th Ave — E 12th Ave
E 13th Ave
W 13th Ave
W 14th Ave — E 14th Ave
W 15th Ave — E 15th Ave
W 16th Ave — E 16th Ave
W 17th Ave — E 17th Ave
W 18th Ave — E 18th Ave
W 19th Ave — E 19th Ave
W 20th Ave — E 20th Ave
W 21st Ave — E 21st Ave
W 22nd Ave — E 22nd Ave
W 23rd Ave — E 23rd Ave
E King Edward Ave
Peveril Ave
Talisman Ave
E 26th St
Hillcrest Park
E 28th St
E 29th Ave

Guelph Park

E Broadway

Kingsway

South Main

Alberta St
Manitoba St
Ontario St
Scotia St
Brunswick St
Guelph St
St George St
Fraser St
Quebec St
Sophia St
Columbia St
James St
Quebec St
Prince Edward St
St George St
Dinmont Ave

400 m
0.2 miles

◎ SEE

◎ OLYMPIC ATHLETES VILLAGE

W 1st Ave

A giant new waterfront complex where 2010 Olympic athletes will be housed, the 'village' is actually a series of swanky condo towers destined to become a new Vancouver neighborhood of several thousand residents after the Games. A great starting point for a seawall stroll to Granville Island, ask locals about the development and they'll regale you with tales of massive cost overruns.

🛍 SHOP

Starting at the 20th Ave intersection, Main St is Vancouver's indie shopping capital. You'll find an afternoon's worth of hipster browsing among the city's pale and interesting set. Of course, you'll never be quite as cool as them, but it's worth a try. See p19 for a summary of what's here.

◻ FRONT & COMPANY
Clothing, Collectibles

☎ 604-879-8431; www.frontandcompany.ca; 3772 Main St; ⏰ 11am-6pm; 🚌 3

A triple-fronted store covering all the bases; the largest section here contains trendy consignment clothing (where else can you find that vintage velvet smoking jacket?). Next door houses new, knowingly cool housewares, while the third area includes must-haves such as manga figures, clockwork toys and nihilist chewing gum (flavorless, of course).

◻ JEM GALLERY *Gallery*

☎ 604-879-5366; 225 E Broadway; ⏰ 11am-5pm Tue-Sat; 🚌 3

Presenting kitsch outsider art from western Canada, the JEM (it stands for Just East of Main) is an unassuming storefront gallery where exhibitions can range from local veteran Jim Cummins' latest painted surfboards to Calgarian Lisa Brawn's cleverly ironic pop-culture woodcuts. Check out the back room, with its tempting prints, jewelry and curios priced to go.

◻ LAZY SUSAN'S *Accessories*

☎ 604-873-9722; 3647 Main St; ⏰ noon-6pm Mon-Sat, noon-5pm Sun; 🚌 3

An eccentric Aladdin's cave lined with tempting trinkets such as Scrabble tile earrings, reproduction old-school greeting cards and obsolete ties transformed into coin purses, it's hard to walk away from here without buying that kitsch-perfect gift for someone back home – possibly a cactus-shaped teapot or a brooch resembling a palm tree.

MOUNTAIN EQUIPMENT CO-OP *Outdoor Equipment*
☎ 604-872-7858; www.mec.ca; 130 W Broadway; 🕙 10am-7pm Mon-Wed, 10am-9pm Thu & Fri, 9am-6pm Sat, 11am-5pm Sun; 🚍 9

Western Canada's favorite outdoor store, MEC is a pilgrimage spot for locals looking for great-quality own-brand clothing, kayaks, sleeping bags and clever camping gadgets. You'll have to be a lifetime member to buy here, but that's easy to arrange and only costs $5. Equipment rentals are also offered and there are several smaller gear stores clustered nearby.

RED CAT RECORDS *Music*
☎ 604-708-7422; www.redcat.ca; 4307 Main St; 🕙 11am-7pm Mon-Sat, 11am-6pm Sun; 🚍 3

The perfect store for tapping the local scene, Red Cat is owned and operated by local musicians Dave Gowans and Lasse Lutick. Their *High Fidelity*–style store is packed with rare and regional CDs and vinyl, and one of them is usually on hand to offer pointers on who to see live and where – you can buy gig tickets here, too.

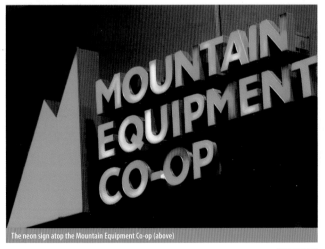

The neon sign atop the Mountain Equipment Co-op (above)

NEIGHBORHOODS

SOUTH MAIN (SOMA)

☐ REGIONAL ASSEMBLY OF TEXT *Stationery*

☎ 604-877-2247; www.assemblyoftext.com; 3934 Main St; ☿ 11am-6pm Mon-Sat, noon-5pm Sun; ☒ 3

Despite sounding like a Soviet government ministry, this eclectic stationery store brims with Little Otsu journals, painted pencil boxes and the kind of handmade greeting cards beloved of eye-rolling ironists. Slip into your fave manila-colored shirt and join the monthly letter-writing club (7pm, first Thursday of every month) to hammer out a missive or two on a vintage typewriter.

☐ SMOKING LILY *Clothing*

☎ 604-873-5459; www.smokinglily.com; 3634 Main St; ☿ 11am-6pm Mon-Sat, noon-5pm Sun; ☒ 3

Quirky art-school cool rules here, with skirts, belts and halter-tops whimsically accented with prints of ants, skulls or the Periodic Table.

Men's clothing is slowly creeping into the mix, with fish, skull and tractor T-shirts and ties. It's hard to imagine a better souvenir than a silk tea cozy printed with a Pierre Trudeau likeness.

☐ TWIGG & HOTTIE *Clothing*

☎ 604-879-8595; www.twiggandhottie.com; 3671 Main St; ☿ 11am-6pm Mon-Sat, 11am-5pm Sun; ☒ 3

Just across from Smoking Lily and named after owners Glencora Twigg and Christine Hotton, this wood-floored nook showcases distinctive garments (plus idiosyncratic jewelry) from Canadian designers: it's *the* place to find something that nobody else is wearing back home. If you're in a budgeting mood, peruse the Steals and Deals rack at the back.

☖ EAT

Good-value ethnic and indie eateries abound along Main St. If

PORTOBELLO WEST MARKET

This monthly indoor **market** (www.portobellowest.com; Rocky Mountaineer station, 1755 Cottrell St; admission $2; ☿ noon-6pm last Sun of the month Mar-Dec; Ⓜ Main St-Science World) showcases distinctive local artists and fashion designers. You'll find hand-painted boots, striking original photography, unique ceramics and just about everything else in between. To get here from the Main St-Science World SkyTrain station, walk east along Terminal Ave to Cottrell St. Turn right and the venue — the Rocky Mountaineer train station — is just head of you. Alternatively, there's a free market shuttle from the corner of Station St and Terminal Ave (in front of Cloverdale Paints; Map p65, C6). It runs every 20 minutes for the duration of the market.

your stomach says time is of the essence, there are many options radiating from the Main and Broadway intersection.

ARGO CAFÉ *Cafe* $
☎ 604-876-3620; 1836 Ontario St; mains $6-10; ⏰ 7am-4pm Mon-Fri; 🚌 3
Fronted by a jaunty painted exterior that suggests you're entering a youth club, the Argo is one of Vancouver's last genuine diner-style cafes. Vinyl booths, a warm welcome and heaping, home-cooked nosh (this is an especially good breakfast spot) are part of its charm and you'll be joined by an eclectic mix of manual workers and in-the-know office drones.

CHUTNEY VILLA *Indian* $$
☎ 604-872-2228; www.chutneyvilla .com; 147 E Broadway; mains $8-18; ⏰ 11:30am-10pm Mon & Wed-Thu, 11:30am-11pm Fri & Sat; 🚌 9
Expect a hug from the owner when entering this warm South Indian restaurant that lures savvy regulars with its lusciously spiced curries (the lamb poriyal is a favorite), often served with fluffy dosas to mop them up. There's an outstanding Sunday brunch combo of veggie curries and piping-hot Indian coffee, plus a drinks list of bottled Indian beers, on-tap BC brews and fresh lime cordial.

The display of clothing and accessories at Twigg & Hottie (opposite) is practically a work of art

FOUNDATION *Vegetarian* $$
☎ 604-708-0881; 2301 Main St; mains $6-14; ⏰ 5pm-1am; Ⓥ; 🚌 3
This lively vegetarian (mostly vegan) noshery is where artsy students and chin-stroking young intellectuals like to hang out. Despite the clientele, it's not at all pretentious (apart from the philosophical quotes adorning the walls) and its mismatched Formica tables are often topped with dishes such as finger-licking nachos or mango and coconut pasta. Vancouver's Storm Brewing beers are also served.

🍴 LIBERTY BAKERY
Cafe $

☎ 604-709-9999; 3699 Main St; snacks $2-4, mains $4-7; ⏱ 8am-5pm; 🚌 3

A handy respite from shopping, the treats at this folksy neighborhood favorite look like they were handmade by a team of expert grandmothers. Try to choose from the bewildering array of fluffy lemon cakes, jaunty gingerbread men and bird's-nest shortbread cookies topped with strawberry jam or simply grab a grilled panini sandwich for lunch. If it's sunny, head for an outside table and watch the Main St bustle.

🍴 THREE LIONS CAFÉ
Gastropub $$

☎ 604-569-2233; 1 E Broadway; mains $8-16; ⏱ 11am-12:30am Tue-Fri, 9am-12:30am Sat & Sun; 🚌 9

'Cafe' doesn't do justice to this relatively new but old-style-feeling spot that's a laid-back neighborhood eatery by day and a cozy pub by night. You'll find a gastropub spin put on Brit classics such as steak-and-Guinness pie, and sausage and mash served in a Yorkshire pudding, plus arguably Vancouver's best hangover-busting weekend breakfast. Drinks include the cafe's own-label lager and canned London Pride.

🍴 SLICKITY JIM'S CHAT & CHEW *Comfort Food* $$

☎ 604-873-6760; 2501 Main St; mains $7-14; ⏱ 9am-7pm Mon-Fri, 9am-5pm Sat & Sun; 🚌 3

A great spot for a heaping weekend brunch, served with the kind of coffee that puts hairs on your tongue, the decor here is a study in hoarded eccentricity, from empty birdcages to dodgy velour portraits (is there any other type?). Snag a table and eavesdrop on the hangover talk from SoMa locals who can't quite remember who they shagged last night.

🍸 DRINK

The intersection of Main and Broadway offers several great independent coffee shops, but there are also bars and other java joints strung far and wide further along Main.

🍸 CASCADE ROOM *Bar*

☎ 604-709-8650; www.thecascade.ca; 2616 Main St; ⏱ 4pm-midnight Mon-Fri, noon-midnight Sat & Sun; 🚌 3

The hopping evenings here make this the best SoMa bar to chat with local hipsters. Gather some Dutch courage with a drinks list ranging from cool cocktails to imported beers (Anchor Steam is recommended) then unleash your slickest lines. Whatever happens, follow the maxim on the glass

WHAT'S SO 'MAIN' ABOUT MAIN ST?

Colonizing the southeast slope above False Creek, SoMa is part of the wider Mount Pleasant district. This district, Vancouver's original suburb, saw the city's first streetcars rattling up the incline here from downtown in 1890. The area became so heavily populated and built-up that it almost became a separate town a few years later – which explains the grand naming of thoroughfares such as Main St, Kingsway and Broadway and the presence of several classic landmark buildings. Regional economic decline triggered a local depression and paint-peeled obsolescence, though, and it wasn't until the 1990s that the area was resurrected as a trendy new 'hood.

panel at the entrance: Keep Calm and Carry On.

☒ GENE CAFÉ *Coffee Shop*
☎ 604-568-5501; 2404 Main St; ☼ 6:30am-11pm; ☒ ☒ 3

Occupying a slender, flatiron wedge of concrete floors and expansive windows, slide onto a chunky cedar bench here with your well-thumbed copy of *L'Etranger* and you might catch the eye of a SoMa local. If not, console yourself with a perfectly baristaed cappuccino and a chunky home-baked cookie (the fruit pies are recommended for additional consolation) at this independent coffeehouse.

☒ WHIP *Bar*
☎ 604-874-4687; www.thewhiprestaurant.com; 209 E 6th Ave; ☼ noon-midnight Tue-Sat; ☒ 3

The art-lined Whip fuses the best in pub and lounge approaches. There's a dare-inviting selection of martinis, each named after a deadly sin (lust is recommended) plus good comfort nosh such as yam *frites* and pad thai. But it's the beer that wins regulars, with choice drafts from R&B Brewing, Storm Brewing and Quebec's scarily strong Unibroue. Sunday's guest keg event is a local legend.

★ PLAY

☒ BILTMORE CABARET
Nightclub, Live Music
☎ 604-676-0541; www.biltmorecabaret.com; 395 Kingsway; cover $5-10; ☒ 9

One of Vancouver's best alt venues has only been open a few years, but it's already a firm favorite. Locals come for a nightly smorgasbord of indie bands that can range from the Wintermitts to Vivian Girls and Attack in Black (what do you mean you've never heard of them?). When there are no bands, burlesque, DJ and film nights keep things lively.

>COMMERCIAL DRIVE

Perched at a tiny street-side table sipping a perfect espresso made by a middle-aged Italian who's clearly having a steamy affair with his beautiful vintage Gaggia is possibly the best way to relax on a Vancouver summer afternoon.

But the city's independent coffee-shop capital has much more to offer than great java. Colonized from the 1950s by generations of European immigrants and later by young counter-culture locals who added a bohemian élan, 'the Drive' offers quirky shops, one-of-a-kind restaurants and friendly bars where quality brews (rather than generic suds) are the main offering. The antithesis of most high streets with their samey chain stores, it could easily be called the 'anti-Robson,' since it couldn't be more different to Vancouver's mainstream thoroughfare. From downtown, alight at the Broadway SkyTrain station and stroll north along Commercial Dr to Venables St and back again for the full effect.

COMMERCIAL DRIVE

🏠 SHOP
Barefoot Contessa 1 C5
Bibliophile Bookshop 2 C5
Dutch Girl Chocolates ...3 C2
La Grotta Del
  Formaggio 4 C4
Urban Empire 5 C3

🍴 EAT
Havana 6 C3
Lime 7 C3

The Reef 8 C2
Theresa's 9 C3
WaaZuBee Café 10 C4

🍸 DRINK
Café Calabria 11 C4
Café Deux Soleils 12 C5
Prado Café 13 C4
Stella's Tap & Tapas
  Bar 14 C3
Timbre 15 C5

⭐ PLAY
Cultch 16 D2
Grandview Bowling
  Lanes 17 C5
Rio Theatre 18 C6
Van East Cinema 19 C6

E Hastings St

To Hastings Park (1km);
Pacific Coliseum (1km);
Playland (1km)

E Pender St

Ferndale St

Turner St

Frances St

Georgia St

Woodland
Park

Georgia St

Adanac St

Venables St

Parker St

Napier St

William St

Grandview
Park

Charles St

Kitchener St

Victoria
Park

Grant St

Graveley St

E 1st Ave

E 2nd Ave

E 3rd Ave

E 4th Ave

E 4th Ave

McSpadden Ave

McSpadden
Park

E 5th Ave

E 5th Ave

E 6th Ave

E 7th Ave

E 8th Ave

See South Main (SoMa)
Map p77

VCC - Clark

Vancouver
Community
College

E 8th Ave

E Broadway

Commercial Drive

Broadway

SHOP

Every store is different here, so a stroll along Commercial's main drag can easily take several hours as you peruse indie pit stops offering everything from used books to handmade chocs and one-of-a-kind fashions.

BAREFOOT CONTESSA
Clothing

☎ 604-255-9035; 1928 Commercial Dr; 🕙 11am-6pm; 🚌 20

The newer satellite store of one of Main St's popular fashion mainstays, the Contessa is all about ladies' wear for those who don't want to be a clone of a chain-store mannequin. You'll find cute hats, frocks and tops from Canadian and international designers, plus a wall of sparkling baubles guaranteed to brighten up any rainy day.

BIBLIOPHILE BOOKSHOP
Bookshop

☎ 604-254-5520; 2010 Commercial Dr; 🕙 11am-6pm; 🚌 20

Serving the area's well-read bohemians, this great used-tome store is one of several bookish nooks along the Drive. Floor-to-ceiling stacks bulge with titles covering just about every subject, including a surprisingly good selection of

An autumn scene along Commercial Dr (p84)

Canadian fiction. The shop additionally sells a menagerie of folk art, which explains the random carved ornaments populating spots where books won't fit.

🏠 DUTCH GIRL CHOCOLATES
Confectionery

☎ 604-251-3221; 1002 Commercial Dr; 🕑 11am-6pm Mon-Sat, noon-5pm Sun; 🚼 ; 🚌 20

This creaky-floored little store is packed with irresistible, house-made confectionery. Nibble on milk-, white- or dark-chocolate models of cars or tennis racquets, peruse sticky jars of liquorice sweeties or select a box of truffles and bonbons from the cabinet. Visiting Netherlanders pining for home can also pick up their fave-branded Dutch candies.

🏠 LA GROTTA DEL FORMAGGIO *Deli*

☎ 604-255-3911; 1791 Commercial Dr; 🕑 9am-5pm Mon-Sat, noon-5pm Sun; 🚌 20

A holdover from the Drive's 'Little Italy' days, this legendary deli is a firm city favorite. Beneath the blue-sky-painted ceiling, you'll find a lip-smacking cheese selection (hence the sweaty sock aroma) plus a wall of marzipan, olive-oil and cream-cracker treats. Gather a picnic and scoff the lot in nearby Grandview Park (right).

COMMERCIAL'S CHATTY GREEN SPACE

The community hub of Commercial Dr is **Grandview Park** (Map p85, C3), between William St and Charles St. A good pit stop for an alfresco coffee or an impromptu picnic, this small, tree-lined area is often buzzing with families and the occasional busker on balmy summer days. It's not hard to see where the park's name comes from – there are great cityscape and North Shore mountain vistas from here – but the tranquil spot also has a surprising military provenance. Originally home to an Irish Fusiliers drill hall, it now houses a slender granite war memorial. Wreaths are laid here on Remembrance Day.

🏠 URBAN EMPIRE *Collectibles*

☎ 604-254-4700; www.urbanempire .ca; 1108 Commercial Dr; 🕑 11am-6pm Mon-Sat, noon-5pm Sun; 🚌 20

This wacky, all-out-kitsch trinket shop is just the kind of place to pick up that Crazy Cat Lady action figure you've always wanted. Other must-haves include bacon-strip sticking plasters and dog-butt-flavored chewing gum – so you'll have no problems finding souvenirs for everyone back home.

🍴 EAT

Eclectic and ethnic eateries abound on Commercial Dr. There's also a healthy bar scene where food is always on offer if you want to soak up the booze.

HAVANA *Latin* $$

☎ 604-253-9119; www.havanarestau rant.ca; 1212 Commercial Dr; mains $10-20; ⏰ 11am-11pm Mon-Thu, 10am-midnight Fri, 9am-midnight Sat & Sun; 🚌 20

The Drive's most popular eatery (especially for its patio) has a menu that combines rustic Latin American dishes with satisfying Afro-Cuban-Southern treats, ranging from finger-licking yam fries to slow-roasted lamb curry and hearty platters of clams, mussels and oysters. Port, brandy and single malt color the drinks list but mojito pitchers are the way to go.

LIME *Japanese* $$

☎ 604-215-1130; www.limerestaurant .ca; 1130 Commercial Dr; tapas $5-16; ⏰ 5pm-1am; 🚌 20

This excellent mod Japanese joint has become a hit with local sushi and sashimi nuts hungry for treats such as scallop, shrimp and snow-crab sunomono. Alongside the raw, there are hearty soba noodle dishes, some cool Asian cocktails and live music on most nights.

THE REEF *Caribbean* $$

☎ 604-568-5375; www.thereefrestau rant.com; 1018 Commercial Dr; mains $11-17; ⏰ 11am-11pm Sun-Wed, 11am-noon Thu & Fri, 10am-noon Sat; 🚌 20

With its kaleidoscope-bright interior, this is a perfect rainy-night spot (which could be any time of the year in Vancouver). The Caribbean soul-food menu includes warming dishes such as Bajan fried chicken and eye-poppingly spicy Jamaican curries. Cocktails are a specialty (try the Dark & Stormy) and all are also available booze-free.

THERESA'S *Comfort Food* $

☎ 604-676-1868; www.theresaseatery .com; 1260 Commercial Dr; mains $4-8; ⏰ 8am-2pm Mon & Tue, 8am-7pm Wed-Sun; 🚌 20

This homely cooperative-run joint (just the kind of commie spot you'd expect on Commercial) gives the counter-culture approach to life a good name. Expect hearty, great-value organic dishes such as orange and ginger pancakes for breakfast plus heaping salad and sandwich combos for lunch. Coffee is fair trade and there's a quiz night the first Wednesday of the month.

WAAZUBEE CAFÉ *International* $$

☎ 604-253-5299; www.waazubee .com; 1622 Commercial Dr; mains $8-20; ⏰ 11:30am-midnight; 🚌 20

Bohemian WaaZuBee's is lined with huge painted murals, velvet curtains and recycled metal sculptures – check out that spoon chandelier. An equally eclectic menu (including plenty of vegetarian options) runs from sesame tuna sashimi to grilled portobello mushroom burgers and maple-soy wild salmon. There's also a good selection of British Columbia beers, including Storm Scottish Ale, made just down the road.

A relaxing moment in the Havana eatery (opposite)

☒ DRINK

A pilgrimage destination for coffee fans – hence the steaming java mugs artfully stenciled into the sidewalks – there are also some great bars here for traveling booze hounds.

☒ CAFÉ CALABRIA *Coffee Shop*
☎ 604-253-7017; 1745 Commercial Dr;
🕙 8am-5pm Mon-Sat, 10am-5pm Sun;
🚌 20

Topping a beanbag of excellent Drive cafes founded by Italian immigrants, this place has guys that really know their java. Don't be put off by the chandeliers-and-statues decor – if Liberace had opened a cafe, this is what it would look like – just order an espresso and biscotti and pull up a chair at this independent coffee shop (see p20 for more info). Java heaven.

☒ CAFÉ DEUX SOLEILS *Cafe*
☎ 604-254-1195; 2096 Commercial Dr;
🕙 8am-midnight; 🚌 20; Ⓜ Broadway

Relax outside this rambling bohemian joint with a Black Plague stout or a fair-trade coffee, or duck inside for evenings of acoustic musicians and open-mike wannabes – the regular poetry slams are a highlight. There's a menu of good-value vegetarian snacks and hearty meals (weekend brunch recommended). Good spot for chilling with the counterculture locals.

☿ PRADO CAFÉ *Coffee Shop*
☎ 604-255-5537; 1938 Commercial Dr;
☺ 6am-8pm; ♿ ; 🚌 20
A hipster reinvention of the Drive's trad coffee shops, the white-washed, minimalist interior of the Prado lures locals craving wi-fi and who like sitting in a corner working on their epic novels in peace. The superb coffee is of the fair-trade variety and is served with artfully patterned foam – add a Nutella chocolate cookie for sustenance.

☿ STELLA'S TAP & TAPAS BAR
Bar
☎ 604-254-2437; www.stellasbeer.com; 1191 Commercial Dr; ☺ 11am-11:30pm Mon-Fri, 10:30am-11:30pm Sat & Sun; 🚌 20
With an eye-popping selection of European (especially Belgian) brews, this is Vancouver's best spot to taste-test draft Leffe, Kronenbourg and Bellevue Kriek – the dark and moody XO is also recommended. Connoisseurs should dive into the fresh sheet of Belgian microbrews, but don't blame us when you wake up the next day with a death-grip hangover.

☿ TIMBRE *Bar*
☎ 604-215-7515; www.timbrerestau rant.com; 2068 Commercial Dr; ☺ 4pm-midnight Mon-Fri, 11am-midnight Sat & Sun; 🚌 20 Ⓜ Broadway

YOU THINK THEREFORE YOU ARE
If the Vancouverites you meet seem too laid-back to engage in hearty debate, head to the **Philosopher's Café** (☎ 778-782-5215; www.sfu.ca/phi losopherscafe; locations vary; admission free-$5), a popular series of engaging discussions staged at restaurants, cafes and galleries across the city. Each night has a different theme – past topics have included 'Is faith an indicator of morality?' and 'Love and romance myths' – and you can sit back and listen to the theories or wade in with your own choice ideas about how things are or ought to be. Check online for times and locations.

This wood-floored corner bar filled with chatter is an ideal spot to meet the locals over a few choice brews (Wednesday's $14 burger and beer night is recommended). There's live jazz on many weekend nights and it's also one of the area's most popular hearty brunch venues.

☆ PLAY
☆ CULTCH *Theater*
☎ 604-251-1363; www.thecultch.com; 1895 Venables St; tickets $5-30; 🚌 20
More properly known as the Vancouver East Cultural Centre, this recently renovated and highly beloved local-performance space is called the Cultch by everyone. Check ahead to see what's on and

you'll find a hugely varied roster of live music, dance and theater from across Canada and around the world.

⭐ GRANDVIEW BOWLING LANES *Activity*

☎ 604-253-2747; 2195 Commercial Dr; 🚶 ; 🚌 20 Ⓜ Broadway

For a cheap and cheerful night out and a retro reminder of the kind of old-school, community venue that used to dot the city, slip into your silver rental shoes and hit the lanes here for some innocent fun. Mostly five-pin, a couple of lanes are also set up for 10-pin fans. It's family-friendly, and the $5 beer and hot-dog combo is a perfect side.

⭐ RIO THEATRE *Cinema, Theater*

☎ 604-878-3456; www.riotheatre.ca; 1660 E Broadway; Ⓜ Broadway

This 1938-built one-screen cinema was sumptuously restored and reopened in 2006 and now offers an eclectic roster of irregular blockbuster movies and carefully chosen special screenings including Friday-night classic horror flicks. The venue is also used for live-music shows and even poetry slams and live theater. Check the website to see what's a'comin'.

⭐ VAN EAST CINEMA *Cinema*

☎ 604-251-1313; www.vaneast.net; 2290 Commercial Dr; tickets adult/child $8/5.50; Ⓜ Broadway

This balconied old neighborhood favorite screens an eclectic schedule of critically acclaimed new and art-house movies (plus second-run blockbusters to keep the money rolling in), with occasional late-night screenings and special events such as movie-maker lectures. Balcony seats are $1 extra and Tuesday tickets are all $5.50.

DETOUR: HASTINGS PARK

Continue north on Commercial Dr then turn right along E Hastings St and within 15 minutes you'll be at Hastings Park. Home of the annual **Pacific National Exhibition** (p26) as well as the popular **Hastings Park Racecourse** (☎ 604-254-1631; www.hastingsracecourse .com), the highlight here is **Playland** (☎ 604-253-2311; www.pne.ca/playland) amusement park. You'll find the usual corkscrew, log flume and battered dodgem rides, plus one of North America's most celebrated old-fashioned roller coasters. The 50-year-old wood-built behemoth powers passengers up a steep incline before letting gravity take over to fling them up, down and around a rickety-feeling track. With a slender bar barely holding you in place, you'll feel like you're in a pinball machine.

>GRANVILLE ISLAND

Vancouver's favorite sunny-afternoon hangout – especially if you like poking around shops rather than communing with nature – this former industrial area (it's a peninsula rather than an island) is the perfect place to lose yourself. The reclaimed factory sheds are now colonized with alluring arts and crafts studios and you'll be serenaded by buskers as you stroll the back alleys and seafront walkways – be sure to arrive or depart on a mini ferry and check out the houseboats at the eastern end for the full 'island' effect.

The highlight attraction is the Public Market, the best in the city, but there are plenty of additional reasons to unleash your itchy credit cards. And be sure to arrive hungry: Granville Island is stuffed to bursting point with indulgent nosh, from market-deli treats to laid-back coffee shops and vista-hugging restaurants.

GRANVILLE ISLAND

◉ SEE
Charles H Scott
  Gallery ....(see 1)
Emily Carr University **1** C4
Granville Island
  Brewing **2** B4
Water Park **3** A4

◻ SHOP
Edie Hats ....(see 6)
Gallery of BC Ceramics **4** B4

Granville Island Tea
  Company ....(see 7)
Kids Market **5** A4
Net Loft ....(see 6)
Oyama Sausage ....(see 7)
Paper-Ya **6** B2
Public Market **7** B2

◻ EAT
Agro Café **8** C4
Bridges **9** A2
Dockside Restaurant ...**10** D4

Edible BC ....(see 7)
Go Fish **11** A4

★ PLAY
Arts Club Theatre
  Company **12** B2
Backstage Lounge .....(see 12)
Ecomarine Ocean Kayak
  Centre **13** A3
Granville Island Stage (see 12)
Vancouver TheatreSports
  League ....(see 12)

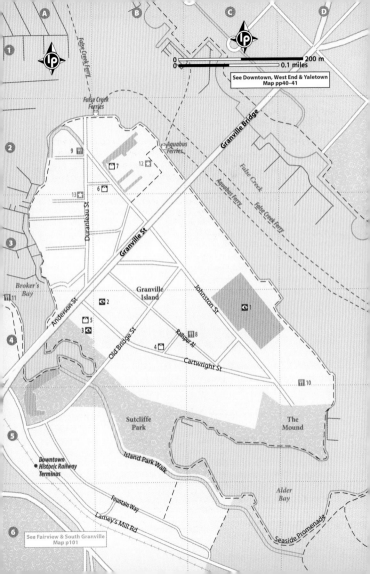

See Downtown, West End & Yaletown
Map pp40–41

A
B
C
D

1

0   200 m
0   0.1 miles

False Creek Ferry

False Creek
Ferries

2

9

7

12

6

13

*Aquabus
Ferries*

Granville Bridge

Aquabus Ferry

False Creek Ferry

False Creek

3

Duranleau St

Granville St

*Broker's
Bay*

11

4

Anderson St

2

Granville
Island

Johnston St

1

5

3

Old Bridge St

Railspur Al

8

4

Cartwright St

10

The
Mound

5

Sutcliffe
Park

*Downtown
Historic Railway
Terminus*

Island Park Walk

*Alder
Bay*

6

Fountain Way

Lamey's Mill Rd

Seaside Promenade

See Fairview & South Granville
Map p101

◉ SEE

While there are several must-see sights here, the best way to experience the island is to wander around and get a bit lost.

◉ EMILY CARR UNIVERSITY

☎ 604-844-3800; www.eciad.ca; 1399 Johnston St; 🕙 10am-6pm; 🚌 50

Vancouver's leading art school occupies a clutch of corrugated metal buildings. There's a good arty bookstore near the main entrance plus annual portfolio shows where you might just catch the work of the next Warhol-like big thing. The free-entry **Charles H Scott Gallery** (☎ 604-844-3811; www.chscott .eciad.ca; 🕙 noon-5pm Mon-Fri, 10am-5pm Sat & Sun) hosts exhibits year-round.

◉ GRANVILLE ISLAND BREWING

☎ 604-687-2739; www.gib.ca; 1441 Cartwright St; tours $9.75; 🕙 tours noon, 2pm & 4pm 🚌 50

Established here in 1984, Canada's oldest microbrewery has mostly shifted production to larger premises but it still makes some of its small-batch brews (including the excellent and alcoholic Ginger Beer) here. The recommended tour walks you through the process before depositing you in the Taproom for some generous sampling. Don't miss the hoppy Brockton IPA, then pick up some takeout.

POTTED PAST

A bustling enclave of rivet and cement manufacturers in the early 1900s, this landfill-created False Creek peninsula was named Mud Island and Industrial Island until the name Granville Island (mirroring the ironwork bridge looming above) eventually took hold.

The area's little businesses were slammed by the Great Depression and a grubby 1930s shantytown gradually took over much of the island, which declined even further after World War II. Industry never fully returned – today's busy cement factory is the only working reminder – but the area received a second lease on life when it was transformed into a highly successful center for artisan studios and theater spaces in the 1970s.

◘ SHOP

It's not just about the Public Market here. There are dozens of artsy stores and galleries radiating across the island, making for an easy hour or two of strollable window shopping. You'll find some of the best spots along Cartwright St, Railspur Alley and in the Net Loft across from the market. For a summary, see p13.

◘ EDIE HATS *Accessories*

☎ 604-683-4280; www.ediehats .com; Net Loft; 🕙 10am-7pm Mon-Fri, 9:30am-7pm Sat & Sun; 🚌 50

Squeeze into this cozy and convivial jungle of classic and contemporary headgear, and try on a few panama hats and a couple of rainbow-colored toques (if you have to ask what a toque is, they'll know you're not Canadian). Staff are ever-friendly and have an irregular habit of handing out choccies if they like the look of you.

GALLERY OF BC CERAMICS
Gallery
☎ 604-669-5645; www.bcpotters.com; 1359 Cartwright St; ◷ 10am-5pm; 🚌 50
The public face of the Potters Guild of BC exhibits and sells the striking works of its member art-

ists, often at excellent prices. You can pick up one-of-a-kind ceramic tankards or swirly painted rustic teapots but look out for the quirky ramen-noodle cups, complete with holes for chopsticks.

KIDS MARKET
Toys, Confectionery
☎ 604-689-8447; www.kidsmarket .ca; 1496 Cartwright St; ◷ 10am-6pm; 👶 ; 🚌 50
This two-story mini mall for under-10s is bristling with kid-friendly stores, mostly of the toy variety. If your sprog's interests extend beyond Lego and Barbie, there are also clothing, candy, magic tricks and arts and crafts hawkers.

Settling in to sample a few brews at the Granville Island Brewing company (opposite)

Deborah Mercier
Co-owner of Granville Island Tea Company in the Public Market

How many cups of tea do you drink per day? Eight. **Recommended tea for travelers** Masala chai. **Best foodie treats around the Public Market** Berry crisp, French pastries, exotic fruits (especially mangoes and pineapples) and ginger and lavender-infused honey from Edible BC (p165). **Tips for first-time Granville Island visitors** Head to the courtyard near the market for the buskers; shoot pictures of the sailboats from the boardwalk; and take one of the little ferries (p99) to English Bay then walk the seawall. **Favorite Vancouver activities** We have our own small plane so we like to flight-see over the city. We also like the theaters and strolling the seawall – I can happily do that anytime. I like visiting the Vancouver Art Gallery (p42), and the aquarium (p60) is always great if you have younger company.

Parents tired of repeated 'buy me this' demands should sneak across to Granville Island Brewing for a restorative libation. If that doesn't work, try the **water park** nearby.

🛍 PAPER-YA *Stationery*
☎ 604-684-2531; www.paper-ya.com; Net Loft; ⏰ 10am-5pm Mon-Sat, 11am-5pm Sun; 🚌 50

A magnet for slavering stationery fetishists (you know who you are), this treasure trove of writing-related ephemera ranges from natty pens to quirky, hand-crafted greeting cards. In between, you'll find an intriguing undercurrent of kitsch-cool Japanese journals and reams of sumptuous washi paper. It's a store that makes you long for the return of traditional letter writing.

🏬 PUBLIC MARKET *Market, Homewares*
☎ 604-666-6477; www.granvilleisland.com; cnr Johnston & Duranleau Sts; ⏰ 9am-7pm; 🚌 50

Granville Island's biggest lure, this indoor deli, produce and crafts cornucopia is often packed in summer – plan to arrive just after opening and you'll enjoy it a whole lot more. Highlight stalls include Oyama Sausage, and Granville Island Tea Company, but there's also an ever-changing array of artisan stands hawking

everything from landscape photography to hand-knitted baby hats. Traveling foodies should take a market tour with Edible BC (p165).

🍴 EAT
You'll need to have your stomach stapled to avoid stuffing your face here. The Public Market is full of treats, while cafes and restaurants pop up around almost every corner calling your name like a siren's song.

🍴 AGRO CAFÉ *Cafe* $
☎ 604-669-0724; www.agrocafe.org; 1363 Railspur Alley; mains $6-10; ⏰ 8am-6pm Mon-Fri, 9am-6pm Sat & Sun; ♿ ; 🚌 50

Seemingly known only to locals, this slightly hidden-away cafe is a smashing coffee stop with a fair-trade commitment. But there's much more on offer here: tuck into a BC-brewed Back Hand of God Stout or a bulging ciabatta sandwich. And if you're hungry for breakfast, the heaping Organic Brekkie is a hearty treat (and a genuine good deal).

🍴 BRIDGES *West Coast* $$
☎ 604-687-4400; www.bridgesrestaurant.com; 1696 Duranleau St; mains $12-24; ⏰ 11am-10pm; 🚌 50

This bright, banana-yellow bistro could serve as Granville Island's

GRANVILLE ISLAND

lighthouse but it's also a longtime foodie fixture that keeps the regulars happy. They come back for the expansive patio views of Burrard Bridge and the North Shore mountains, served with standard comfort food classics such as chicken quesadillas, fish-and-chips and hearty thin-crust pizzas (the smoked-salmon variety is recommended).

🍽 DOCKSIDE RESTAURANT
West Coast $$

☎ 604-685-7070; www.dockside brewing.com; 1253 Johnston St; mains $14-26; ⏱ 7am-10pm; 🚌 50
Wood-grilled steaks, mint-crusted lamb and butter-soft wild salmon are the highlights at this convivial dining room and brewpub combo adjoining Granville Island Hotel. If it's raining, you can hunker inside the woodsy main room, but sunny days mean snagging a table on the chatty waterfront patio. Brewpub faves include Alder Bay Honey Lager.

🍽 GO FISH *Seafood* $

☎ 604-730-5040; 1505 W 1st Ave; mains $8-13; ⏱ 11:30am-6:30pm Wed-Fri, noon-6:30pm Sat & Sun; 🚌 50
Tucked along the seawall west of Granville Island, this seafood shack serves excellent fish and chips, with cod, salmon or halibut. The great (and lighter) fish tacos

are also recommended, while ever-changing specials – sourced from wharfside fishing boats – can include scallop burgers or ahi tuna sandwiches. Pack your nosh to nearby Vanier Park for a breezy picnic.

⭐ PLAY

There's more than shopping and eating to keep you occupied on the island, including live comedy, music and theater – plus kayaking and mini-ferry trips.

⭐ ARTS CLUB THEATRE COMPANY *Theater*

☎ 604-687-1644; www.artsclub.com; Granville Island Stage; tickets $30-60; 🚌 50 ⛴ Granville Island (Aquabus)
Musicals, international classics and works by contemporary Canadian playwrights are part of the mix of one of the city's top theater companies. If you're curious about West Coast theater, look out for plays by Morris Panych, BC's favorite playwright son. And if you've got kids in tow, check the company's Spring Break Theatre Festival, a week of live sprog-friendly performances.

⭐ BACKSTAGE LOUNGE
Live Music

☎ 604-687-1354; www.thebackstage lounge.com; 1585 Johnston St; ⏱ noon-2am Mon-Sat, noon-midnight Sun; 🚌 50 ⛴ Granville Island (Aquabus)

MINI FERRY SHUFFLE

Anyone can walk onto Granville Island via the Anderson St main entrance (Map p93, A4) but arriving in style means taking one of the bathtub-sized ferries plying the waters of False Creek. Running vessels (some big enough to carry bikes) between the foot of Hornby St (Map p93, C1) and Granville Island, **Aquabus Ferries** (☎ 604-689-5858; www .theaquabus.com; adult/child from $3/1.50) services spots along the waterfront as far as the Olympic Village and Science World. Its fierce rival is **False Creek Ferries** (☎ 604-684-7781; www.granvilleislandferries.bc.ca; adult/child from $3/1.50), which operates a similar Granville Island service from the Aquatic Centre (Map pp40–1, B6), plus other ports of call around False Creek. Both operators offer day passes at the same prices (adult/child $14/8), but if you forget to pay they might make you walk the plank.

If the sun is setting and you're looking for a little action, head to this laid-back waterfront bar where live local music hits the stage every night. Expect an eclectic array of singer-songwriters, cover bands and the odd kick-ass indie group, plus a side order of ever-changing drinks specials, often featuring Granville Island Brewing.

⭐ ECOMARINE OCEAN KAYAK CENTRE *Activity*
☎ 604-689-7575, 888-425-2925; www .ecomarine.com; 1668 Duranleau St; rentals 2/4hr $36/60; ◷ 9am-6pm Sun-Thu, 9am-9pm Fri & Sat Jun-Aug, 10am-6pm Sep-May; 🚌 50
There's no better way to catch the spirit of Vancouver than a gentle paddle around the glassy-calm coastline of False Creek, with the city's signature skyline towers winking at you from the shore. The friendly folk here can rent you gear or take you out for a convivial two- to four-hour guided tour (from $59).

⭐ VANCOUVER THEATRESPORTS LEAGUE *Theater*
☎ 604-738-7013; www.vtsl.com; New Revue Stage, 1585 Johnston St; tickets from $10.50; ◷ Wed-Sat; 🚌 50 🚇 Granville Island (Aquabus)
The city's enduring improv troupe stages energetic romps loosely connected to themes such as Shakespeare, *Star Trek* or the 2010 Olympics. If you're sitting near the front, expect to be picked on and possibly called into the spotlight, where you'll likely be mercilessly laughed at. Curl into a fetal position in a corner of the stage and they might leave you alone.

>FAIRVIEW & SOUTH GRANVILLE

While clamorous W Broadway is lined with shops and restaurants, it's never been the kind of destination street its name implies. This West Side strip is too long to have a single identity, with the vastly different neighborhoods it passes through claiming sections of it as their own. And so it is with artsy South Granville and the residential old Fairview neighborhood, both of which are worth an afternoon trawl.

South Granville St – optimistically named South Granville Rise by PR bods trying to spin the uphill climb from the Granville Bridge – is lined with browsable independent galleries, chic boutiques and some excellent restaurants between W 4th and W 16th Aves. Fairview – named for the sterling views of mountain-backed downtown from its stepped slopes – includes an art deco city hall, some attractive heritage homes and the city's second most popular park; the only area in these neighborhoods where you're likely to run into tourists.

FAIRVIEW & SOUTH GRANVILLE

◉ SEE
Bloedel Floral Conservatory	1	C5
City Hall	2	D2
Queen Elizabeth Park	3	D5
VanDusen Botanical Garden	4	B6

🛍 SHOP
Bacci's	5	A2
Bau-Xi Gallery	6	A3
Equinox Gallery	7	A2
Meinhardt Fine Foods	8	A3

🍴 EAT
Bin 942	9	A2
Ouisi Bistro	10	A3
Paul's Place Omelettery	11	A2
Rangold	(see 13)	
Tojo's	12	B2
Vij's	13	A2
West	14	A2

★ PLAY
Nat Bailey Stadium	(see 16)	
Stanley Theatre	15	A2
Vancouver Canadians	16	D5
Vancouver Olympic Centre	17	D5

See Kitsilano
Map p109

See Granville Island
Map p93

See Downtown, West End & Yaletown
Map pp40–41

See Gastown & Chinatown
Map p65

W 1st Ave
W 2nd Ave
W 3rd Ave
W 4th Ave
W 5th Ave
W 6th Ave
W 7th Ave
W 8th Ave
W Broadway
W 10th Ave
W 11th Ave
W 12th Ave

W 1st Ave
W 2nd Ave
W 3rd Ave
W 4th Ave
W 5th Ave
W 6th Ave

Olympic Village

Fairview

Jonathan
Rogers Park
W 8th Ave
W Broadway
W 10th Ave
W 11th Ave
W 12th Ave
W 13th Ave
W 14th Ave
W 15th Ave
W 16th Ave

Broadway
City Hall

False Creek Ferry

Alder
Bay

Charleston
Park

W 6th Ave

Lamey's Mill Rd

Commodore Rd

Pine St
Fir St
Granville St
Hemlock St
Birch St
Alder St
Spruce St
Oak St
Laurel St
Willow St
Heather St
Ash St
Cambie St
Yukon St
Alberta St

South
Granville

Vancouver
General
Hospital

W 14th Ave
W 15th Ave
W 16th Ave

McRae Ave
Tecumseh Ave

Shaughnessy
Park

Wolfe Ave

W 17th Ave
W 18th Ave
W 19th Ave
W 20th Ave
W 21st Ave
W 22nd Ave
W 23rd Ave

See South Main
(SoMa)
Map p77

South
Main

Columbia St
Manitoba St

Matthews Ave

Hudson St
Selkirk St
Oster St

Balfour Ave

Laurier Ave

W King Edward Ave

Douglas Park

W 24th Ave

W 26th Ave
W 27th Ave
W 28th Ave
W 29th Ave

King Edward

Nanton Ave
Devonshire Cr
Connaught Dr

Granville St

Devonshire
Park

W 32nd Ave

Oak St

BC Children's
Hospital

Heather St

Braemar
Park

Dinmont Ave
Peveril Ave
Hillcrest
Park

Midlothian Ave

Queen
Elizabeth
Park

Ontario St

W 33rd Ave

33rd Ave
(Proposed)

VanDusen
Botanical
Garden

Kersland Dr

Queen Elizabeth
Pitch & Putt Golf
Course

W 37th Ave

W 37th Ave

To Richmond
Oval (8km)

0   700 m
0   0.4 miles

W 39th Ave
W 40th Ave

SEE

Fairview hosts some of Vancouver's most popular park attractions, while South Granville is all about the shop-and-gallery-lined stroll from the bridge to W 16th Ave.

BLOEDEL FLORAL CONSERVATORY

☎ 604-257-8584; www.vancouverparks.ca; Queen Elizabeth Park; adult/youth/child $4.80/3.35/2.40; ☻ 9am-8pm Mon-Fri, 10am-9pm Sat & Sun May-Aug, 10am-5pm Sep-Apr; 👶; 🚌 15

Duck inside the centerpiece of tree-lined Queen Elizabeth Park, a triodetic dome for 500 plant varieties and dozens of tropical birds (including a chatty cockatoo) in three walk-through, climate-controlled environments. Back outside, climb the steps to your right and you'll come to a large synchronized fountain plus an imposing Henry Moore bronze that has a twin in London's Kew Gardens.

CITY HALL

☎ 604-873-7011; www.vancouver.ca; 453 W 12th Ave; admission free; ☻ 8:30am-5pm Mon-Fri; Ⓜ Broadway-City Hall

Fans of art deco should save time for a stroll though the marble-lined lobby of one of Vancouver's best architectural gems, completed in 1936. Its highlights include a mirrored ceiling, streamlined signs, cylindrical lanterns and embossed elevator doors. Duck inside one of the elevators to peruse its intricate inlaid wood design, then check out the handsome heritage homes on surrounding Yukon St and W 12th Ave.

QUEEN ELIZABETH PARK

☎ 604-257-8584; www.vancouverparks.ca; cnr Cambie St & W 33rd Ave; 🚌 15

Accessed via the Cambie St and W 33rd Ave entrance (bus 15 stops right outside), this is Vancouver's second main urban green space. Conceived as a beautification project to cover an old quarry,

SWANK SHAUGHNESSY

If you're coming along Granville St from the airport, pry your jet-lagged eyes open and you'll spot some extremely large heritage mansions hidden behind the towering hedges. When you're later ambling along South Granville checking out the shops, continue to W 16th Ave, turn left, and then make a sharp right up McRae Ave. Within a couple of minutes, you'll be in the leafy heart of Shaughnessy Heights. Planned as a fat-cats neighborhood for the wealthiest Vancouverites in the early 1900s, it's still lined with magnificent old piles that make it a wanderable museum of architectural styles. Look out for everything from revivalist Tudor and Georgian to colonial Dutch and Spanish, then buy a lotto ticket so you can move right in.

Autumn is a fabulous time to explore Queen Elizabeth Park (p102)

there's a pair of immaculately coiffured landscaped areas suffused with flowers and shrubs plus some of the city's best hilltop views of mountain-backed Vancouver.

◉ VANDUSEN BOTANICAL GARDEN

☎ 604-878-9274; www.vandusengar den.org; 5251 Oak St; adult/youth/child $8.85/6.50/4.70; ⊗ 10am-5pm Mar & Oct, 10am-6pm Apr, 10am-8pm May, 9am-9pm Jun-Aug, 10am-7pm Sep, 10am-4pm Nov-Feb; 🚌 17

A highly ornamental confection of sculptures, Canadian heritage flowers, rare international plants and a popular Elizabethan hedge maze, VanDusen is also one of Vancouver's top Christmas destinations, complete with thousands of twinkling fairy lights. The annual June Garden Show is also a highlight.

🏠 SHOP

South Granville Rise (from Granville Bridge to W 16th Ave) is lined with independent galleries and browsable boutique shops. In contrast, the W Broadway stretch of Fairview is a grab bag of mostly mainstream and neighborhood stores.

FAIRVIEW & SOUTH GRANVILLE

DON'T MENTION THE TRAINS...

While Cambie St is a model of organized bustle today, the area has only just begun recovering from construction of the Canada Line, which opened in 2009. The mostly underground line – there's a station at W Broadway and Cambie St if you want to check it out – was built using a cheaper but highly disruptive cut-and-cover technique that turned much of the street into an open trench for two years. Not surprisingly, locals avoided the chaotic area, subjecting area shops and eateries to business Siberia. Many struggled, a few relocated and some simply gave up and closed down, sometimes after operating here for decades. Perhaps worried about setting a precedent, the provincial government refused all compensation claims.

BACCI'S *Clothing, Homewares*
☎ 604-733-4933; www.baccis.ca; 2788 Granville St; 🕑 9:45am-5pm Mon-Sat; 🚌 10

Combining designer women's clothing on one side and a room full of hard-to-resist trinkets piled high on antique wooden tables on the other, Bacci's is a dangerous place to browse. Before you know it, you'll have an armful of chunky luxury soaps, embroidered cushions and picture-perfect coffeepots to fit in your suitcase.

BAU-XI GALLERY *Gallery*
☎ 604-733-7011; www.bau-xi.com; 3045 Granville St; 🕑 10am-5:30pm Mon-Sat, noon-4pm Sun; 🚌 10

One of the long-established galleries responsible for the city's artistic renaissance in recent years, Bau-xi (pronounced 'bo-she') showcases the best from local artists and generally has prices to match its exalted position. The main gallery selection changes monthly and the focus is usually on original paintings, although prints, drawings and sculpture are also part of the mix on occasion.

EQUINOX GALLERY *Gallery*
☎ 604-736-2405; www.equinoxgallery.com; 2321 Granville St; 🕑 10am-5pm Tue-Sat; 🚌 10

Another veteran of the South Granville scene, Equinox focuses on quality contemporary works from established Canadian and international artists. Some of the leading lights continually on offer are Jack Shadbolt, Fred Herzog and Liz Magor and, along with paintings, there's a commitment to sculpture and provocative installations.

MEINHARDT FINE FOODS *Deli*
☎ 604-732-4405; www.meinhardt.com; 3002 Granville St; 🕑 9am-9pm Mon-Sat, 9am-8pm Sun; 🚌 10

The culinary equivalent of a sex shop for fine-food fans, the narrow aisles at this swanky deli and grocery emporium are lined with international condiments, luxury canned goods and the kind of tempting treats that everyone should try at least once. Drop by for global Christmas goodies or build your perfect picnic from the tempting bread, cheese and cold-cuts selections.

🍴 EAT

South Granville has several excellent midrange and higher-end dining options, especially south of the W Broadway intersection. The W Broadway stretch of Fairview is dotted with good-value, family-run eateries plus a few unexpected surprises.

🍴 BIN 942 *International*　　　$$

☎ 604-734-9421; www.bin941 .com; 1521 W Broadway; tapas $12-15; 🕑 5pm-2am; 🚌 9

This slender, cozy nook is one of Vancouver's best late-night options if you crave shareable dishes and a wind-down drink or three with chatty friends. Consider 'Tapatisers' such as sashimi-style ahi tuna or portobello mushroom cutlets, along with some lip-smacking beer (Russell Brewing Cream Ale is recommended) or a glass from the compact wine list of Australian, Californian, European and local tipples.

🍴 OUISI BISTRO *Cajun*　　　$$

☎ 604-732-7550; www.ouisibistro.com; 3014 Granville St; mains $9-22; 🕑 11am-1am Mon-Fri, 9am-1am Sat & Sun; 🚌 10

Vancouver's best creole and Cajun soul-food joint, Ouisi (as in 'Louisiana') chefs up adventurous dishes such as habanero coconut chicken, cornmeal-crusted trout and vegetarian étouffée for those who like a taste-tripping dinner. The large menu of accompanying malts and bourbons plus regular live jazz spices things up, while weekend brunch offers hot-fusion riffs on trad breakfast dishes.

Tojo in the restaurant (p106) named after himself

🍴 PAUL'S PLACE OMELETTERY
Comfort Food $$

☎ 604-737-2857; 2211 Granville St; mains $8-12; ⏰ 7am-3pm; 👶 ; 🚌 10

This is one of the city's fave breakfast and brunch spots for in-the-know locals (especially those living across the street in those shiny new condos). The menu specializes in hearty, perfectly prepared omelets (the Da Vinci, made with chorizo sausage and wild game, is recommended). Hearty lunchtime dishes, including burgers and sandwiches, are also available.

🍴 TOJO'S *Japanese* $$$
☎ 604-872-8050; www.tojos.com; 1133 W Broadway; mains $19-26; ⏰ 5-10pm Mon-Sat; 🚌 9

Long-regarded as Vancouver's best sushi joint, swank Tojo's doesn't disappoint. Favored dishes include lightly steamed monkfish, sautéed halibut cheeks and fried red tuna wrapped with seaweed and served with plum sauce. Seats at the sushi bar are much sought-after, so reserve as early as possible, then celebrate with a selection or two from the excellent sake menu.

🍴 VIJ'S *Indian* $$$
☎ 604-736-6664; www.vijs.ca; 1480 W 11th Ave; mains $18-26; ⏰ 5:30-10pm; 🚌 10

This contemporary Indian restaurant fuses local ingredients, global flourishes and classic recipes to produce unique dishes such as wine-marinated 'lamb Popsicles' or halibut, mussels and crab tomato-ginger curry. The adventurous should try the *paranta*: flat breads made with roasted ground crickets. Reservations are not accepted, so if you're in a hurry, decamp to Rangoli, the adjoining takeout cafe.

🍴 WEST *West Coast* $$$
☎ 604-738-8938; www.westrestaurant.com; 2881 Granville St; mains $24-42; ⏰ 11:30am-2pm Mon-Fri, 5:30-11pm nightly; 🚌 10

The chef who made this place an award-winning favorite is gone but standards remain exceptionally high in a kitchen specializing in seasonal Pacific Northwest treats such as Okanagan lamb and Maple Hill chicken. The service here is possibly the city's best, with a warm, snob-free approach that makes you feel instantly welcome – ask for wine recommendations and you'll find the staff really know their stuff. It's a perfect dine-out for a special occasion.

⭐ PLAY

There's just enough to keep you occupied here, including a popular live-theater venue and some lively sports attractions.

⭐ STANLEY THEATRE *Theater*
☎ 604-687-1644; www.artsclub.com; 2750 Granville St; tickets $30-60; 🚌 10

A heritage, 1931-built satellite venue of the Arts Club Theatre Company, this picturesque 1200-seat auditorium stages professional, mostly mainstream plays and musicals for its loyal regulars. Check out some of the building's art deco and Moorish architectural flourishes, including an odd little turret on the top outside.

⭐ VANCOUVER CANADIANS *Sporting Venue*
☎ 604-872-5332; www.canadians baseball.com; Nat Bailey Stadium, 4601 Ontario St; tickets $8-14; 🕐 regular season Jun-Sep; 🚴 ; 🚌 3

A sunny afternoon at the old-style Nat Bailey Stadium with the Vancouver Canadians (Oakland Athletics affiliate) is less about watching great baseball and more about cold beer and a fistful of salty pretzels. Afternoon games – called 'nooners' – are perfect for a family-friendly, nostalgic bask, complete with sigh-triggering North Shore mountain vistas. The 2010 Olympics has triggered a long-overdue stadium revamp.

ROCK & ROLLER

The city's newest and arguably most entertaining spectator sport, **Terminal City Rollergirls** (www.terminal cityrollergirls.com; tickets $15-20) is an all-female flat-track roller-derby league with teams comprising local ladies who don bad-ass personas as soon as they strap on their roller skates. Their fast-paced matches – among teams with names such as Riot Girls and Bad Reps – are quite possibly the most fun you'll ever have at a sporting event in Vancouver. Venues vary around the city, so check the league's website for fixtures.

⭐ VANCOUVER OLYMPIC CENTRE *Sporting Venue*
4574 Clancy Loranger Way; 🚴 ; 🚌 3

Home of the 2010 Olympic and Paralympic curling events, this brand-spanking-new 6000-seat Hillcrest Park facility has eight ice sheets that came at a cost of a cool $38 million. After the Games, it will become a state-of-the-art public curling facility and a multi-use community center for the area (a new swimming pool facility has been built alongside to wow the locals).

>KITSILANO

A former hippie enclave where the flower children grew into large mortgages and professional jobs, 'Kits' is now one of Vancouver's most attractive older neighborhoods. Named after Chief Khahtsahlanough, leader of a First Nations village that occupied the seafront stretch latterly designated as Vanier Park, the area is lined with preserved wooden heritage homes, many of which are among the city's most sought-after properties. During the 1960s, these airy Craftsman piles were colonized by counterculture locals who fueled political movements such as Greenpeace and edgy newspapers such as the *Georgia Straight*, now Vancouver's top listings rag.

For visitors, the main Kits attractions are the sandy string of rustic beaches that offer some of the region's best sunset views, as well as the shopping and dining options that line W 4th Ave and W Broadway, the area's two main thoroughfares. It's the perfect laid-back escape from the clamorous streets of downtown.

KITSILANO

👁 SEE

🛍 SHOP

🍴 EAT

⭐ PLAY

NEIGHBORHOODS

KITSILANO

⊙ SEE

Waterfront Vanier Park is home to a triumvirate of Vancouver museums and the Kitsilano shoreline has several popular beach hangouts. See p17 for a summary of the beaches here.

⊙ HASTINGS MILL STORE MUSEUM

☎ 604-734-1212; north foot of Alma St; admission by donation; ⏱ 11am-4pm Tue-Sun mid-Jun–mid-Sep, 1-4pm Sat & Sun mid-Sep–mid-Jun; 🚌 4

Constructed in 1865, Vancouver's oldest still-standing building was originally located near Gastown, where it served workers at one of the region's first sawmills. Surviving the 1886 fire, it was barged here in the 1930s and is now a little museum of eclectic artifacts, pioneer-era photos and First Nations exhibits.

⊙ HR MACMILLAN SPACE CENTRE

☎ 604-738-7827; www.hrmacmillan spacecentre.com; 1100 Chestnut St, Vanier Park; adult/youth/child $15/10.75/10.75; ⏱ 10am-5pm, closed Mon Sep-Jul; ♿ ; 🚌 22

Beloved of galloping school groups (try to get here early), the center offers plenty of hands-on action, from alien battles to spacecraft design and simulator

Vanier Park (p111) is a great place for a picnic

rides to Mars. For older kids and kitsch-loving adults, the planetarium stages laser shows (tickets $10.75) synchronized to the music of Coldplay, Led Zeppelin and Pink Floyd (*Dark Side of the Moon* never looked better).

⊙ JERICHO BEACH PARK

north foot of Wallace St; 🚌 4

An idyllic escape from downtown, this tree-fringed park space is fronted by an expansive, log-studded beach, where you can drink in spectacular seaside sunsets. It's a popular jogging spot, and you can also stroll east along the waterfront from here: look out for the Marginal Wharf, an old promenade that stands on piles over the brine. Kayaking and windsurfing are available here.

📷 KITSILANO BEACH PARK

cnr Cornwall Ave & Arbutus St; 🚌 22
More crowded than Jericho Beach, the area's fave sunny-day hangout, the wide, sandy curve of Kits Beach is often littered with drowsy sunbathers, shouting Frisbee tossers and giggling volleyball nuts. Facing English Bay, it has great views of the city framed by the looming mountains. There's a saltwater swimming pool if you don't want to hit the waves, and a large park restaurant.

📷 MUSEUM OF VANCOUVER

☎ 604-736-4431; www.museumof vancouver.ca; 1100 Chestnut St, Vanier Park; adult/child $11/7; 🕙 10am-5pm Tue-Sun, 10am-7pm Thu Jul & Aug, closed Mon Sep-Jun; ♿ ; 🚌 22
Housed in a modernist building shaped like a Coast Salish hat, the museum offers temporary exhibitions on topics such as Stanley Park's social history and the Vancouver school of architecture, while continuing to showcase the city's timeline, pop-culture past and First Nations heritage.

📷 VANCOUVER MARITIME MUSEUM

☎ 604-257-8300; www.vancouver maritimemuseum.com; 1905 Ogden Ave, Vanier Park; adult/child $10/7.50; 🕙 10am-5pm mid-May–Aug, 10am-5pm Tue-Sat, noon-5pm Sun Sep–mid-May; ♿
The highlight of the landmark A-frame building is the *St Roch*, an arctic patrol vessel that was the first to navigate the Northwest Passage in both directions. Also check outside for the *Ben Franklin*, a NASA research submarine used for a record-breaking 30-day dive in 1969. The collection may be moved to a proposed North Vancouver maritime center, so check ahead.

📷 VANIER PARK

via Chestnut St from intersection with Cornwall Ave; 🚌 22
A waterfront park attracting joggers and kite flyers in almost

---

MUSEUMS ON THE CHEAP

Bring a picnic and spread out on the grass in Vanier Park, then take in all three of the nearby museums with a budget-saving **Explore Pass**. Covering the **HR Macmillan Space Centre** (opposite), **Vancouver Maritime Museum** (above) and **Museum of Vancouver** (above), it costs $30 (saving $6 on separate entry fees) and is available at the front desk of all three attractions.

equal numbers, this area was once a First Nations settlement. Aside from the three museums here, look out for the window-like artwork that frames a picture-perfect view of the North Shore mountains. Great for a picnic, it's also just a 15-minute seawall stroll southeast to Granville Island (p92).

🛍 SHOP

W Broadway and W 4th Ave are Kitsilano's main thoroughfares and each is lined with stores, book-stores and restaurant pit stops. Check www.kitsilano4avenue.com for shopping suggestions.

🏠 GRAVITY POPE *Clothing*
☎ 604-731-7673; www.gravitypope .com; 2205 W 4th Ave; ⏱ 10am-9pm Mon-Fri, 10am-7pm Sat, 11am-6pm Sun; 🚍 4
One of a clutch of cool Kits clothing stores, this unisex shop includes hipster footwear and designer togs for the pale-and-interesting set (think ironic tweed ties and printed halter tops). Don't spend all you dosh here, though: check out nearby Vivid and Urban Rack, too.

🏠 KIDSBOOKS *Books, Toys*
☎ 604-738-5335; www.kidsbooks.ca; 3083 W Broadway; ⏱ 9:30am-6pm Mon-Thu & Sat, 9:30am-9pm Fri, 11am-6pm Sun; 🧒 🚍 9

Like a theme park for bookish kids, Canada's largest children's bookshop stocks thousands of novels, picture books, history titles and anything else you can think of to keep them quiet. Check ahead for regular events and readings by visiting authors, plus a selection of toys and games.

🏠 KITSILANO FARMERS MARKET *Market*
☎ 604-879-3276; www.eatlocal.org; Kitsilano Community Centre, 2690 Larch St; ⏱ 10am-2pm Sun mid-Jun–mid-Oct; 🚍 9
One block south of W Broadway along Larch St, the Kitsilano Com-munity Centre is home to this popular summer-long market, where you'll find luscious regional fruits including plums, peaches and apples (depending on the season), plus BC cheeses, baked treats and a few craft-stall diver-sions. Bring a bag and fill up.

🏠 ZULU RECORDS *Music*
☎ 604-738-3232; www.zulurecords .com; 1972 W 4th Ave; ⏱ 10:30am-7pm Mon-Wed, 10:30am-9pm Thu & Fri, 9:30am-6pm Sat, noon-6pm Sun; 🚍 4
It's easy to waste a rainy after-noon here sifting the racks of new and used vinyl and CDs, including hard-to-find imports, in search of that obscure album by the long-forgotten Pathetic Flowers.

Drop into a listening booth to try before you buy and ask the staff for local band recommendations – they sell tickets to many area shows.

🍴 EAT

Instead of foraging for food on the beaches here, check out W Broadway, W 4th Ave and beyond for some excellent Kits eateries.

🍴 BISHOP'S *West Coast* $$$
☎ 604-738-2025; www.bishopsonline.com; 2183 W 4th Ave; mains $28-38; ⏲ 5:30-11pm; 🚌 4

Long before 'locavore' dining became de rigueur, John Bishop was serving smoked West Coast sablefish, Fraser Valley duck confit and the kind of crisp, seasonal veggies that tasted as if they'd been plucked from the ground that morning. Little has changed at the city's coziest fine-dining joint, where Bishop often stops by the tables for a chat.

🍴 EATERY *Japanese* $$
☎ 604-738-5298; www.theeatery.ca; 3431 W Broadway; mains $7-16; ⏲ 4:30-11pm Mon-Thu, 4:30pm-midnight Fri, 12:30pm-midnight Sat, 12:30-11pm Sun; Ⓥ; 🚌 9

Wooden booths and lava lamps are all part of the kitsch ambience at this pop-culture reinvention of a trad sushi joint. Bring your manga comic and dive into the enormous menu of soba bowls, curry-rice and sushi combos, washed down with a Japanese beer. Non-meat options abound, including share-able platters for those vegetarians traveling in packs.

🍴 FUEL *West Coast* $$$
☎ 604-288-7905; www.fuelrestaurant.ca; 1944 W 4th Ave; mains $24-34; ⏲ noon-2:30pm Mon-Fri, 5:30-10:30pm daily; 🚌 4

Despite the bland name, this celebrated Kits eatery sources exceptional regional ingredients and transforms them with a knowing cosmopolitan flair. Everything is

WHERE SAVING THE PLANET BEGAN...

Along the seawall between Granville Island and Vanier Park, around the foot of W 1st Ave, cast your eyes to the sidewalk and you'll find a small, unassuming plaque that almost everyone walks past without noticing. It marks the spot where, in 1971, a fledgling local activist group called the Don't Make a Wave Committee set sail to Alaska on board a chartered boat to protest against US nuclear testing. Intercepted by the American navy, the vessel never reached its destination. But the bearded Kitsilano-based activists were inspired to keep pursuing causes and they changed their name to Greenpeace the following year.

seasonal, so expect regular menu changes – if you're lucky, glazed Fraser Valley lamb will be on. If not, console yourself with some Buckwheat honey crème brûlée.

☷ LUMIÈRE *International* $$$
☎ 604-739-8185; www.lumiere.ca; 2551 W Broadway; mains $24-36, prix fixe tasting menus from $98; ⏲ 5:30-11pm Tue-Sun; 🚌 9

With Iron Chef Rob Feenie's 2008 departure, few thought this award-winning eatery would survive. But New Yorker superstar Daniel Boulud rolled in and reinvented the top-notch eatery with exquisitely executed dishes such as slow-baked arctic char and Redbro chicken stuffed with truffles. The menu comprises multicourse tasting selections intended for savoring – this is not so much a dinner as an event.

☷ NAAM *Vegetarian* $$
☎ 604-738-7151; www.thenaam.com; 2724 W 4th Ave; mains $8-14; ⏲ 24hr; Ⓥ; 🚌 4

Hardwood floors, rickety tables and a chatty ambience fuel the middle-class hippie feel at Vancouver's favorite vegetarian noshery. The entry queue (especially on weekends) allows time to decide between tofu stir-fries and the recommended sesame fries with miso gravy. There's nightly live music, organic beers and a covered patio for cozying with a bowl of broth on rainy days.

☷ SOPHIE'S COSMIC CAFÉ
Comfort Food $$
☎ 604-732-6810; www.sophiescosmic cafe.com; 2095 W 4th Ave; mains $6-14; ⏲ 8am-9:30pm; 🚶; 🚌 4

Kitsch-lined local legend Sophie's is a happening diner spot with burgers, club sandwiches and big-ass milkshakes dominating the menu – there are also a few unexpected gems such as BC oyster burgers. A highly popular breakfast and brunch spot –

Taking a break in Sophie's Cosmic Café (above)

expect weekend queues – it's also worth dropping by mid-afternoon for some truck-stop coffee and a pyramid-sized slice of apple pie.

⭐ PLAY

Hit the beaches for outdoor activities then spend the evening taking in a movie or rubbing your goateed chin knowingly with some live jazz.

⭐ CELLAR RESTAURANT & JAZZ CLUB *Live Music*
☎ 604-738-1959; www.cellarjazz.com; 3611 W Broadway; cover from $10; 🚌 9
A serious subterranean muso joint, the intimate cellar is known for showcasing hot local performers plus some great touring acts. The atmospheric little corner stage lures aficionados from across the region with a fusion of classic tunes and edgier fare. Check website listings.

⭐ ECOMARINE OCEAN KAYAK CENTRE *Activity*
☎ 604-689-7575; www.ecomarine.com; Jericho Sailing Centre, 1300 Discovery St; 🕐 9am-dusk May-Aug, 9am-dusk Sat & Sun Sep; 🚌 4
The full-moon paddle, back-dropped by twinkling downtown towers and shimmering phosphorescence, is the kind of guided tour ($59) you'll rave about when you get back home. If you miss

it (check the website for dates), there's a plethora of daytime options, lessons for all levels and rentals for those who prefer doing their own thing.

⭐ RIDGE THEATRE *Cinema*
☎ 604-738-6311; www.festivalcinemas .ca; 3131 Arbutus St; tickets adult/youth/child $12/9/8; 🚌 16
A popular neighborhood cinema, this is the perfect place to catch the latest art-house or not-quite-mainstream new release. There's also a smattering of special shows such as filmed operas and family-friendly kid matinees. The Ridge's sister venue **Fifth Avenue Cinemas** (☎ 604-734-7469; www.festivalcinemas .ca; 2110 Burrard St; tickets adult/youth/child $12/9/8; 🚌 44) has more screens and more movie options.

⭐ WINDSURE ADVENTURE WATERSPORTS *Activity*
☎ 604-224-0615; www.windsure.com; Jericho Sailing Centre, 1300 Discovery St; board/skim board rentals per hr $18.58/4.64; 🕐 9am-8pm Apr-Sep; 🚌 4
For those who want to be at one with the sea breeze, Windsure specializes in kiteboarding, windsurfing and skimboarding and offers lessons and equipment rentals. Novices are more than welcome: the two-hour windsurfing introductory group lesson ($49) is highly recommended.

>UNIVERSITY OF BRITISH COLUMBIA (UBC)

With a student populace topping 45,000 and an isolated peninsula location that's quite a hike from the city center, UBC feels more like a separate town than a local school. But it's well worth the trek if you're looking for an off-the-beaten-path half-day out. And once you're here, you can pretend you're still a student by strutting around like the cool undergrad you used to be all those years ago – just don't talk to the real undergrads about Crowded House or Tears for Fears and you might even get away with it.

There's a surprising array of campus attractions to keep you occupied here, including a contemporary art gallery, two celebrated landscaped gardens and arguably the region's best museum. There's also a wanderable treasure trove of intriguing outdoor art. And be sure to peruse the evening options, complete with a couple of performance spaces that should satisfy most culture vultures.

UNIVERSITY OF BRITISH COLUMBIA (UBC)

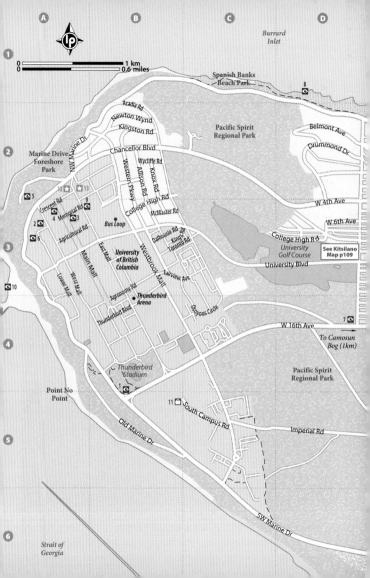

◉ SEE

Many of UBC's main attractions are strung along or around the main University Town thoroughfares of East Mall, Main Mall, West Mall and Lower Mall. See p22 for an overview of the attractions.

◉ BOTANICAL GARDEN

☎ 604-822-9666; www.ubcbotanical garden.org; 6804 SW Marine Dr; adult/youth/child $8/6/free; ☷ 10am-6pm mid-Mar–mid-Oct, 10am-3pm mid-Oct–mid-Mar; ♿ ; 🚍 C20
You'll find a giant collection of rhododendrons, a fascinating apothecary plot and a winter green space of off-season bloomers in this 28-hectare complex of themed gardens. The new 308m-long **Greenheart Canopy Walkway** (☎ 604-822-9666, 888-755-3227; www.greenheartcanopywalkway.com; adult/youth/child $20/14/6; ☷ 9am-5pm) lifts visitors 17m above the forest floor on a guided eco tour. Walkway tickets include garden entry.

◉ MORRIS AND HELEN BELKIN GALLERY

☎ 604-822-2759; www.belkin.ubc.ca; 1825 Main Mall; admission free;

The canopy walkway at UBC's Botanical Garden (above) gets visitors close up to a forest

🕑 10am-5pm Tue-Fri, noon-5pm Sat & Sun; 🚌 99B-Line

This excellent little gallery specializes in contemporary and often quite challenging pieces – which explains the billboard-style depiction of an Iraqi city outside, complete with the caption 'Because there was and there wasn't a city of Baghdad.' Inside, you can expect a revolving roster of traveling shows plus chin-stroking exhibits from a permanent collection of Canadian avant-garde works.

🅞 MUSEUM OF ANTHROPOLOGY AT UBC

☎ 604-822-3825; www.moa.ubc.ca; 6393 NW Marine Dr; adult/child $12/10, $6 after 5pm Tue; 🕑 10am-5pm Wed-Mon, 10am-9pm Tue; 🚌 99B-Line

Recently re-opened after a huge $55 million reno that doubled its size, Vancouver's best museum houses Canada's most important northwest coast aboriginal-artifact collection, including a spectacular array of totem poles. The expansion enables many non–First Nations exhibits to finally see the light of day, including a fine array of Cantonese opera costumes – no, you can't try them on.

🅞 NITOBE MEMORIAL GARDEN

☎ 604-822-6038; www.nitobe.org; 1895 Lower Mall; adult/youth/child $6/2/free; 🕑 10am-6pm mid-Mar–mid-Oct,

PUBLIC ART HUNT

As you wander around the campus, keep your eyes peeled for an alfresco menagerie of intriguing campus art. You should be able to spot the *Victory Through Honour* totem pole near Brock Hall, which includes UBC's famous thunderbird sport team symbol; Rodney Graham's full-size horse carriage in a glass case, entitled *Millennial Time Machine*, not far from the Morris and Helen Belkin Gallery; and a Chinese rock garden near the Asian Centre where the boulders are inscribed with deep-and-meaningful Confucian sayings.

10am-2:30pm Mon-Fri mid-Oct–mid-Mar; 🚌 99B-Line

Exemplifying Japanese horticultural philosophies, this verdant tranquility oasis includes a Tea Garden – complete with ceremonial teahouse – and a Stroll Garden that reflects a symbolic journey through life with its little waterfalls and languid koi carp. Named after Dr Inazo Nitobe, a scholar whose mug appears on Japan's ¥5000 bill, a springtime visit reveals florid cherry-blossom displays.

🅞 PACIFIC SPIRIT REGIONAL PARK

☎ 604-224-5739; cnr Blanca St & W 16th Ave; 🕑 dawn-dusk; 🚌 99B-Line

Larger than Stanley Park, this dense forest is a green moat separating the city from the campus. Lined with 54km of walking, jogging and cycling trails, it's a popular exercise hangout for homework-avoiding students and sporty Kitsilano locals alike. Visit the Park Centre on W 16th Ave for info and ask about the area's **Camosun Bog wetland**, a haven for native bird and plant species.

SPANISH BANKS
NW Marine Dr; 🚌 44

This tree-backed public beach is a popular locals' hangout – the locals are the ones jogging past in Lululemon outfits – as well as being a good spot to unpack a picnic and perch on a log to enjoy some sigh-triggering waterfront vistas. The sandy stretch was named after English Bay's 1792 meeting between British mariner Captain George Vancouver and his Spanish counterpart Dionisio Galiano. You can get there via the Salish Trail from UBC campus, which starts at 41st and Camosun Sts but has additional access points throughout Pacific Spirit Regional Park.

WRECK BEACH
west foot of University Blvd; www .wreckbeach.org; 🚌 C20

Enjoying the tranquility of the Japanese-inspired Nitobe Memorial Garden (p119)

RIOT TIME AT UBC

The campus might be quiet and tranquil on your visit but November 25, 1997 was quite a different matter. Around 2000 protesters flooded in for the annual Asia-Pacific Economic Cooperation (APEC) of world leaders, angered by the presence of what they regarded as 'brutal dictators' and stoked up by police attempts to keep them at bay. The height of the protest occurred around Gate 6 on NW Marine Dr, where police and students clashed as the leaders tried to leave. Barricades were trashed, pepper spray was unleashed and TV images flashed around the world. Four years later, a public inquiry blamed senior police officers for violating the rights of the protesters.

Follow Trail 6 into the woods then head down the steep steps to the water and you'll find Vancouver's only official naturist beach, complete with a motley crew of counterculture locals, independent vendors and sunburned regulars. Threatened in recent years by encroaching UBC housing developments, the story of the underpants-free area is colorfully related in the book *Wreck Beach* by Carellin Brooks.

🛍 SHOP

🛍 UBC FARM MARKET *Market*
☎ 604-822-5092; www.eatlocal.org; 6128 South Campus Rd; snacks from $1; 🕙 9am-1pm Sat Jun-Oct; 🚍 99B-Line
Hawking produce grown right here at the much-loved UBC Farm, this seasonal market offers fresh, mostly organic fruit and veggies to a loyal clientele of locals. The produce is picked on the day (or the day before) the

Saturday sale and, depending on the time of year, can include carrots, tomatoes, melons, peppers and lots of flowers (but try not to eat these).

⭐ PLAY

With such a large population, there's always a busy roster of happenings at UBC. But you don't have to endure a public lecture on thorax variations in South American ants (with accompanying slides) to have a campus-based night out.

⭐ CHAN CENTRE FOR THE PERFORMING ARTS *Live Music*
☎ 604-822-9197; www.chancentre .com; 6265 Crescent Rd; tickets $10-40; 🚍 99B-Line
This dramatic elliptical auditorium is one of Vancouver's best venues for classical-music shows and it's also the new permanent home of the old CBC Radio Orchestra, controversially dumped by Canada's

public TV and radio provider in 2008. The orchestra has since been renamed the National Broadcast Orchestra. Check out the Chan website for details of forthcoming events.

⭐ FREDERIC WOOD THEATRE
Theater

☎ 604-822-2678; www.theatre.ubc
.ca; 6354 Crescent Rd; tickets $14-20;
🚌 99B-Line

The university's trainee luvvies, plus graduate thesps and drama-faculty members, stage some celebrated and professionally slick productions at this campus theater, including well-known classics and also a roster of more challenging fare. The season usually runs from October through to March, with each production lasting around a week and tickets priced to go.

>2010 OLYMPIC & PARALYMPIC WINTER GAMES

The high slopes near Whistler will host the 2010 Olympic & Paralympic Winter Games

2010 OLYMPIC & PARALYMPIC WINTER GAMES

Vancouver will be the world's party central from February 2010, when the Winter Olympic and Paralympic Winter Games finally rolls into town after several years of intense planning, some impressive new venues and more than a little local taxpayer hand-wringing. Costs will be far from the minds of most spectators as they skip giddily between events and partake of a region-wide fiesta that will transform the metropolis for both the Olympics (staged from February 12 to 28) and the Paralympics (from March 12 to 21).

If you're planning to join the five rings and roll in for the sporting trip of a lifetime, keep in mind that events are widely distributed around the region, with Vancouver and Whistler, which is a two-hour drive away on Hwy 99, dividing up the spoils.

Opening and closing ceremonies are staged at downtown's BC Place Stadium (p39), while events in greater Vancouver include snowboard and freestyle skiing at Cypress Mountain (p61); curling at the Vancouver Olympic Centre (p107); figure skating and short-track speed skating at the Pacific Coliseum (off Map p85); speed skating at Richmond Oval (off Map p101); and ice hockey at GM Place (p52) and the new Thunderbird Arena (Map p117, B4).

As 2010's 'host mountain,' Whistler stages alpine skiing events (downhill, super-G, giant slalom, slalom and combined) in its Creekside area; luge, skeleton and bobsleigh events at the purpose-built Whistler Sliding Centre; and Nordic events (biathlon, cross-country skiing, Nordic combined and ski jumping) at a magnificent backcountry location 16km

2010 OLYMPICS FACTS

> 80+ participating countries
> 5500 Olympic athletes and officials
> 1350 Paralympic athletes and officials
> 10,000 media people
> 86 Olympic events
> 64 Paralympic events
> 3 billion global viewers

Canadian athletes are poised to enter BC Place Stadium (p39), where the opening ceremony will be held

from the village called Whistler Olympic Park. Paralympic alpine skiing, cross-country skiing and biathlon will also be staged at these venues. The majority of the 2010 facilities will be accessible to visitors for tours or activities after the Games.

At time of research, tickets (half of which are priced under $100) were selling well and availability will be as scarce as a Mauritian luge gold medalist for main events such as hockey, snowboarding and the opening and closing ceremonies. If you discover you're too late for tickets, consider the Paralympics, where contests are just as fiercely fought and prices and availability are more amenable. Information on buying 2010 tickets is available via the official **Olympics website** (www.vancouver2010.com).

Of course the Olympics isn't just about scoring tickets. Vancouver – which hosts an Athlete's Village on the south bank of False Creek (see p78; ask a local for the financial shenanigans behind it) – has set aside several free gathering places for those who want to feel the Olympic spirit for free. Robson Sq (Map pp40–1, D4) near the Vancouver Art

Gallery is the main party site, hosting athlete demonstrations and live performances. Additional crowd hangouts will be Yaletown's David Lam Park (Map pp40–1, D7), downtown's Larwill Park (Map pp40–1, F5), Granville Island (Map p93) and the Vancouver Public Library (Map pp40–1, E5).

There's also a 60-day Cultural Olympiad from January 22 to March 21, staging 600 concerts and events – many of them free – across the city. Highlight performers will include Robert Lepage, the Alberta Ballet and the Vancouver Symphony Orchestra (p55).

GM Place (p55) is set to give an enthusiastic welcome to Canada's national team at the 2010 Games

MASCOTS A-GO-GO

Recognizing the potential cash cow of a successful Olympic mascot, 2010 Games' organizers aren't relying on a single oddball beast to increase their coffers. Instead, the region's big sporting party is supported by three furry, kid-friendly critters guaranteed to pry open the most reluctant of parental wallets. Miga is a sleek little sea bear which, according to her profile, likes snowboarding and smoked salmon; Sumi is a spikey-hatted animal spirit that enjoys flying and quaffing cocoa; and Quatchi (everyone's secret favorite) looks like a hard-drinking backcountry biker dude but is actually a hairy sasquatch that spends his time playing hockey and eating anything he can get his giant hands on. You can meet the crew at www.vancouver2010/mascots.

If you're planning to commute from Vancouver to Whistler during the Games, be aware that there will be no public parking – only those with confirmed hotel rooms or those who live in the area will be allowed to drive through on Hwy 99 – and spectators will be expected to use public transportation options instead. Olympic buses will run between the city and Whistler and will cost $25 for an all-day pass. Around-the-clock transit vehicles will also operate to move visitors between the Whistler venues. For 2010 transportation information, visit www.translink.bc.ca.

Accommodation in Vancouver and Whistler will be extremely tight for the duration of the Games: consider places in the suburbs as alternatives and book ahead as soon as possible. For sleepover options and Games updates, visit the dedicated webpage of **Tourism Vancouver** (www.tourismvancouver.com). Also check the website of the *Vancouver Sun* (www.vancouversun.com; click on the Vancouver 2010 logo) for up-to-the-minute 2010 info.

Vancouver is a full-on city of many dimensions, with extensive drinking and dining scenes complemented by festivals, outdoor attractions and live-music options that shouldn't be missed by anyone. Whatever your inclination, peruse these pages for ideas on experiencing the Lotusland capital.

Science World at Telus World of Science (p66) and the Omnimax Theatre

SNAPSHOTS

ACCOMMODATIONS

While the 2010 Olympic & Paralympic Winter Games (p123) encourages visitors to think outside the box when it comes to accommodations – staying in a luxe cruise ship is one of the more novel suggestions – at other times Vancouver usually has more than enough hotels, B&Bs and hostels to meet demand. Recent years have also seen several swanky new downtown properties opening, including the boutique **Loden** (www.lodenvancouver.com) and **L'Hermitage** (www.lhermitagevancouver.com) and the elaborate **Shangri-La** (www.shangri-la.com), which resides in the city's tallest building.

If you want to be in the heart of the action and within walking distance of restaurants, bars and shops, the downtown core is lined with the usual chain hotels plus a few recommended independents. These include the top-end **Wedgewood** (www.wedgewoodhotel.com), the midrange **Victorian** (www.victorianhotel.ca) and the newly refurbished **St Regis** (www.stregishotel.com), as well as Yaletown's popular **Opus Hotel** (www.opushotel.com). Alternatively, try the **Urban Hideaway Guesthouse** (www.urban-hideaway.com), a well-priced and particularly cozy home-from-home that's perfectly located in the city center.

You'll find plenty of heritage sleepovers in the West End, where there are some excellent, antique-lined B&Bs plus a few older but well-maintained midrange options, including the charming, ivy-covered **Sylvia Hotel** (www.sylviahotel.com). This area is ideal if you want to be a short walk from the center and Stanley Park, while at the same time enjoying the quietude of a residential neighborhood.

Across False Creek, Kitsilano combines B&Bs with character – many in refurbished Craftsman homes – with a smattering of very handy

lonely planet Hotels & Hostels

Need a place to stay? Find and book it at lonelyplanet.com. More than 50 properties are featured for Vancouver – each personally visited, thoroughly reviewed and happily recommended by a Lonely Planet author. From hostels to high-end hotels, we've hunted out the places that will bring you unique and special experiences. Read independent reviews by authors and other travelers, and get practical information including amenities, maps and photos. Then reserve your room simply and securely via our online booking service. It's all at www.lonelyplanet.com/hotels.

self-catering apartments: you'll be able to chef-up your own nosh, or just amble along W 4th Ave for a dine-out. Further west, the University of British Columbia (UBC) has a wide range of student and higher-end seasonal accommodation.

For those on a budget, downtown's two most popular hostels – **Samesun Backpackers** (www.samesun.com) and **HI Central** (www.hihostels.ca) – face each other across Granville St. The city also has two additional HI hostels in the West End and at Jericho Beach. Perhaps the city's best budget option (aside from sleeping in your car) is downtown's **Hotel St Clair** (www.stclairvancouver.com), a hidden pension-style property with a nautical theme and a good location.

Not surprisingly, July and August – as well as the 2010 Olympics – are peak times for Vancouver accommodation rates, but prices can drop by as much as 50% off-season (May, June and September are recommended). Many hotels also offer good-value packages including restaurant deals, spa treatments or entry to local attractions. Check accommodations and hotel websites for the best deals and tempting packages. Keep in mind that many city hotels charge parking fees of between $10 and $20 per night – avoid this by staying at B&Bs, where parking is usually free.

WEB RESOURCES
2010 Destination Planner (www.2010destinationplanner.com)
Access Vacation Group (www.emrvacationrentals.com)
Hello BC (www.hellobc.com)
Tourism Vancouver (www.tourismvancouver.com)
Western Canada B&B Innkeepers Association (www.wcbbia.com)

BEST STYLISH SLEEPOVERS
> L'Hermitage Vancouver (www.lhermitagevancouver.com)
> Loden Vancouver (www.lodenvancouver.com)
> Metropolitan Hotel (www.metropolitan.com/vanc)
> Opus Hotel (www.opushotel.com)
> Shangri-La Hotel (www.shangri-la.com)

BEST HERITAGE CHARMERS
> Corkscrew Inn (www.corkscrewinn.com)
> Fairmont Hotel Vancouver (www.fairmont.com/hotelvancouver)
> O Canada House B&B (www.ocanadahouse.com)
> Sylvia Hotel (www.sylviahotel.com)
> Victorian Hotel (www.victorianhotel.ca)

FESTIVALS

While July and August are peak months for Vancouver festivals, the city has a year-round roster of events that should give you some entertaining options no matter what time of year you're here. Peruse the Vancouver Calendar (p23) for a wealth of ideas, plus the dates and websites for the following events.

Performance art is heavily represented in festivals here, with the International Fringe Festival (p26) and Bard on the Beach (p25) bringing in the major numbers: the former is a kaleidoscope of short plays and comedy reviews staged around Granville Island (where you can expect to be accosted by performers trying to press-gang you into seeing their show), while the latter is a summer-long run of four Shakespeare (and Shakespeare-related) plays staged in Vanier Park tents. It doesn't get more West Coast than watching an alfresco shoreline performance, with the sun setting over the mountain skyline.

If music is more your bag, summer in the city offers the giant International Jazz Festival (p25) and MusicFest Vancouver (p26), which covers everything from world to classical and back again. While each includes dozens of shows at venues around the city, they also turn Vancouver into party central with free outdoor performances in Gastown, Yaletown and on a temporary stage on the W Georgia St side of Vancouver Art Gallery.

Aside from these mammoth events, there's a long list of smaller, off-the-beaten-path cultural happenings that are well worth a look. Car Free Vancouver (p25), the Powell Street Festival (p25) and the Eastside Culture Crawl (p28) are grassroots fests with a fun local edge – check the *Georgia Straight* website (www.straight.com) for other seasonal happenings taking place during your visit.

Finally, if festivals mean parades to you, the city has three that couldn't be more different. The annual St Paddy's Day CelticFest (p24) includes a leprechaun-friendly procession of bands and wannabe Irish folk; the August Pride (p25) parade brings out the whole city for a gay old time at Vancouver's largest street party; and the massive early-December Santa Claus Parade (p28) includes carriages, sing-alongs, fairy-tale floats and an appearance by the real Santa (we think).

BEST FESTIVALS WITH FREE EVENTS
> Canada Day (p25)
> Car Free Vancouver (p25)
> Celebration of Light (p25)
> CelticFest (p24)
> International Jazz Festival (p25)

BEST ARTS FESTIVALS
> Eastside Culture Crawl (p28)
> MusicFest Vancouver (p26)
> Vancouver International Film Festival (p27)
> Vancouver International Fringe Festival (p26)
> Push (p24)

Top left A grand parade is the highlight of the CelticFest celebrations (p24), which are held around St Patrick's Day

FOOD

If you stepped back in time into a regular 1980s Vancouver restaurant, you'd likely be tucking into a rubbery steak and some overcooked veggies while sipping a glass of fizzy, factory-made beer. Even the Depeche Mode soundtrack playing through your mind wouldn't compensate for this lackluster nosh, which is a good reason to avoid food-based time travel on your next visit.

To say that Vancouver's dining scene has moved on since the '80s is an understatement of sirloin-sized proportions. Arguably edging ahead of Canadian epicurean rivals Montreal and Toronto in recent years, the city's foodie renaissance has been driven on two key fronts: local ingredients and ethnic influences.

Originally enjoyed only by locals at home, Vancouver restaurants have been rediscovering British Columbia's cornucopia of distinctive produce and piquant flavors since the mid-1990s, when it suddenly became fashionable to brag about sourcing your prawns from a nearby sleepy island.

In fact, while pioneers such as Bishop's (p113) and Raincity Grill (p49) used to be lone doyens of delectables including Fraser Valley duck, Salt Spring lamb and Queen Charlotte Islands halibut, locavore ingredients now dominate menus across the city. Naturally, finger-licking West Coast seafood is at the forefront of this taste-tripping approach, ranging from contemporary-cool C Restaurant (p46) to the traditional but mighty Fish House in Stanley Park (p62).

But even without this bounty, Vancouver would be a great dining city based on its smorgasbord of ethnic eateries. Although these were originally aimed at sustaining immigrants salivating for a taste of home, Vancouverites have been discovering these joints for years – it's common to tuck into the best sushi outside Japan at Tojo's (p106), for example, and follow it with a Chinese feast in the evening at Hon's Wun-Tun House (p70). For contemporary Indian, try Vij's (p106); for good comfort Mexican, dip into La Casita (p70); and for fine French dining, head to Le Gavroche (p49).

Top dining streets, where you can't throw a kapamaki roll without hitting a good eatery, include downtown's Robson St; the West End's Denman and Davie Sts; Yaletown's Hamilton St; along Commercial Dr;

and Kitsilano's W 4th Ave. And don't forget the city's bars: many pubs are as much about food as they are about drink, with top-notch gastropub offerings available at joints such as the Irish Heather (p70) and Alibi Room (p71). Their excellent beer selections also help.

If you're more of a wandering gourmand, the city's markets are a great way to tuck into a few treats at the same time as walking off those calories. The Asian summertime Chinatown Night Market (p67) is lined with steaming food stands, while seasonal farmers markets in the West End (p45), UBC (p121) and Kitsilano (p112) are recommended for fresh-picked local fruits and veggies (miss the succulent cherries and lush peaches at your peril). Granville Island Public Market (p97) is the year-round granddaddy of them all, with deli and bakery treats and shiny piles of produce encouraging instant gorging.

If you're finding the choice a little bewildering, there are several ways to save time while you're on the ground. The websites of local print publications the *Georgia Straight* (www.straight.com), *Eat Magazine* (www.eatmagazine.ca) and *City Food* (www.cityfood.com) have handy listings and reviews of area eateries, or you can just pick up the latest newsstand issue. Alternatively, go online and check out **Urban Diner** (www.urbandiner.ca) for the latest news, openings and recommendations.

BEST BREAKFASTS
> Deacon's Corner (p69)
> Ouisi Bistro (p105)
> Paul's Place Omelettery (p106)
> Slickity Jim's Chat & Chew (p82)
> Templeton (p50)

BEST REGIONAL CUISINE
> Bishop's (p113)
> C Restaurant (p46)
> Fuel (p113)
> Raincity Grill (p49)
> West (p106)

BEST BUDGET EATERIES
> Go Fish (p98)
> Gorilla Food (p47)
> Japa Dog (p48)
> Mr Pickwick's (p49)
> Theresa's (p88)

BEST INTERNATIONAL CUISINE
> La Casita (p70)
> Motomatchi Shokudo (p49)
> Tojo's (p106)
> Vij's (p106)

BARS & PUBS

Mirroring Vancouver's lip-smacking restaurant renaissance, there has been a sudsy surge in the city's quality drinking establishments during the last few years. Where creaky neighborhood pubs were once the only spots to grab a tipple (older locals still bemoan the loss of some of these grubby old bars), a wealth of newer watering holes has suddenly sprung up like drunks at an open bar. This could have led to a characterless gentrification of the city's drinking scene, but luckily the opposite has been the case.

Head to Gastown and you'll experience this elevation firsthand. Vancouver's oldest enclave is lined with landmark stone and brick buildings that now house some of the city's best drinking establishments – it's ideal for a pub crawl that will barely graze your knees. In the shadow of the 'Gassy' Jack statue – suitably perched atop a whiskey barrel – you can hit the extensive beer list at brick-lined Six Acres (p73); neck the perfect pint of stout at the chatty Irish Heather (p70); then weave merrily to the Alibi Room (p71) for a taste-trip among 19 on-tap microbrews and three cask ales, most from British Columbia (BC). Accompanying food isn't an afterthought at these bars, with tempting charcuterie plates as the current dish du jour – the Heather even cures its own meat.

The Alibi is the most lip-smacking exemplar of another renaissance in Vancouver's drinking scene. A decade ago, most city bars served generic industrial brews made by factory beer producers such as Labatt and Molson, along with one or two 'exotic' beers from sole local microbrewer

Granville Island Brewing. Now, distinctive BC-brewed tipples are offered at bars around the city: look out for beers by Crannog Ales, Storm Brewing, Phillips Brewing and Central City Brewing, and see the boxed text, p50, for more suggestions.

And don't miss Granville Island. Canada's first microbrewer is still operating after more than two decades. Its new Brockton IPA recently joined the family and its fun brewery tour (p94), complete with several lip-smacking samples, is still a top activity for beer fans. If you're here in the cold season, the rich Winter Ale is highly recommended.

While Gastown is the best Vancouver 'hood for a bar crawl, other pockets of boozy largesse include downtown's Granville Strip, where it's all about partying hard and drinking enough to hit the dance floors; the West End's Davie St, which has several popular gay bars; and Yaletown, where loungey bars for those who don't just want a beer can be easily found.

While brews from across the province are the city's hot-ticket drink these days, Vancouver is surprisingly deficient in dedicated brewpubs. If you like the idea of drinking a beer that was made just a few feet away from your table, you can sup the made-on-site suds at Steamworks Brewing Company (p73), Dix BBQ & Brewery (p50) and Yaletown Brewing Company (p52). And if you're into the kind of ultrastrong Belgian beers that put hairs on your tongue, slide under the table at Stella's Tap & Tapas Bar (p90).

Drinking isn't only about beer of course. The loungier end of the bar spectrum is well represented at watering holes such as the cozy Afterglow (p50) and the weekend-clamorous Cascade Room (p82), where mixing it up with a few classic and exotic cocktails may have you chatting up the wait staff. Just remember: whatever lines you use, they've heard them all before.

BEST BARS FOR FOOD
> Alibi Room (p71)
> Dix BBQ & Brewery (p50)
> Irish Heather (p70)
> Six Acres (p73)
> Three Lions Café (p82)

BEST PATIOS
> Mill Marine (p52)
> Six Acres (p73)
> Stella's Tap & Tapas Bar (p90)
> Yaletown Brewing Company (p52)

Top left Customers enjoy a beer the Yaletown Brewing Company (p52)

SHOPS & MARKETS

While shopping in Vancouver used to involve little more than selecting a thick winter coat or picking up some maple-sugar cookies, the city's retail experience has changed remarkably in recent years. And while familiar chain outlets and department stores are still the city-center mainstay – especially along Robson St – there are some highly browse-worthy shopping enclaves that require a little traveling. If shopping is your thing, it's a trip well worth making.

For hot indie fashion designers, head to the hipster stores of SoMa (p78) or the short Gastown strip of Cordova St between Richards and Cambie Sts. There's also a full shopping list of independents along Kitsilano's W 4th Ave (p112) and plenty of unique and quirky shops on both sides of Commercial Dr (p86). For tips on the latest must-buy items, coolest local stores and latest trends, visit www.vitamindaily.com and www.scoutmagazine.ca.

If you're of the artsy persuasion, head to the studios and artisan workshops of Granville Island (p94) or the private galleries of South Granville (p103) for the kind of souvenir you won't find anywhere else – better than taking home a package of vacuum-packed salmon.

In fact, food shopping is one of the city's best retailing experiences. Whatever the weather, check out the produce and deli delectables on offer at the Granville Island Public Market (p97), where picking up some regional spices, jarred preserves or a bar of chunky chocolate at the Edible BC stand is highly recommended. In summer, you'll find a similar selection at farmers markets around the city, including at UBC (p121), Kitsilano (p112) and the West End (p45). And don't miss the Chinatown Night Market (p67), an atmospheric evening bazaar renowned for its food stands and kitschy trinkets that feels a little like being in Hong Kong.

Wherever you shop, keep in mind that prices on most shop goods do not include tax, which is added when you take the item to the cash register to pay. GST (5%) and PST (7%) taxes are usually added.

BEST BOOKSHOPS
> Bibliophile Bookshop (p86)
> Kidsbooks (p112)
> Little Sisters Book & Art Emporium (p44)
> Sophia Books (p45)

BEST INDEPENDENT CLOTHES SHOPS
> Barefoot Contessa (p86)
> Edie Hats (p94)
> Gravity Pope (p112)
> Smoking Lily (p80)
> Twigg & Hottie (p80)

Top left Fruit stalls at Granville Island's Public Market (p97) **Above** Tea stand at Chinatown Night Market (p67)

LIVE MUSIC

While the biggest acts suck up giant ticket prices at downtown stadium gigs, seeing a band at almost any other Vancouver venue is much more satisfying. The Commodore (p53) is everyone's favorite midsized venue – not just for it's bouncy mosh pit – and it frequently hosts top-class visiting and local acts that don't demand an arm and a leg for entry.

Visiting musos who really want to tap the local scene, though, should dig a little beneath the city surface. You'll find that Vancouver is studded with cool little venues where you can catch up with eclectic out-of-town acts and touch base with a hipsterish local scene.

The hottest local venue at the moment is SoMa's Biltmore Cabaret (p83), where a fairly oddball nightly roster of indie bands, beat poetry, art-house movies and even burlesque acts seeks to lure the local cool crowd away from the coffee shops. The Biltmore follows a similar sched-uling approach to downtown's favorite and long-established alt music venue, the Railway Club (p54).

Tucked inauspiciously upstairs next to a 7-11 store, 'the Rail' combines an old-school, Brit-style bar area (where you can escape the music if it's damaging your brain) with a tiny stage that hosts acts every night. Ron Sexsmith and the Proclaimers have played here over the years (not at the same time, apparently) and it's traditionally been a great spot to catch the next big act before they sell out and hit the stadiums.

It's a 10-minute walk south from here to downtown's other somewhat hidden live venue. The Media Club (p53) is a small, low-ceilinged spot that rarely strays far from its attempts to bring rocking live indie acts to its in-the-know clientele. This is not a place to come and chat, but to dive in and rock.

Check ahead using www.livevan.com to see what's on in the city. You can book tickets through **Live Nation** (www.livenation.com) or **Ticketmaster** (www.ticketmaster.ca), which also provide listings of upcoming events. Pick up a copy of the *Georgia Straight* free weekly (or check www.straight.com) for the latest happenings and reviews. Alternatively, hit Red Cat Records (p79) or Zulu Records (p112) to chat and gather suggestions on who to see. Both shops sell tickets to local shows.

Of course, Vancouver isn't just about rock and roll. Chin-stroking jazz cats should head downstairs at the subterranean Cellar Restaurant & Jazz Club (p115) for an intimate atmosphere and some serious licks. It's even more laid-back at downtown's O'Douls (p52), where this hotel bar is enlivened by free nightly jazz performances. It's the place to be during the city's giant International Jazz Festival (p25), when acts that have performed across the city drop by to jam into the wee hours.

Festivals are a highlight of Vancouver's music scene and should not be missed if you're around. July's Folk Music Festival (p25) draws thousands of alfresco fans to Jericho Beach, while August's giant MusicFest (p26) offers a bewildering variety of genres at free and paid venues across the city. Jazz, opera, world-music and classical fans can usually find more than enough to keep them happy at this three-week-long fiesta.

And if it's classical that floats your boat, the Vancouver Symphony Orchestra (p55) is one of Canada's favorites. Its main venue is downtown's Orpheum Theatre, a sumptuous baroque-revival masterpiece that's arguably Vancouver's best sit-down music venue. Just ask anyone who saw the spine-tingling Tom Waits gig here a few years ago.

BEST LIVE VENUES

> Biltmore Cabaret (p83)
> Malkin Bowl (p63)
> Media Club (p53)
> Orpheum Theatre (p55)
> Railway Club (p54)

BEST MUSIC FESTIVALS

> MusicFest Vancouver (p26)
> Vancouver Folk Music Festival (p25)
> Vancouver International Jazz Festival (p25)

Top left The entrance, complete with beer menu, to the Railway Club (p54)

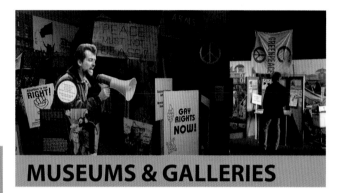

MUSEUMS & GALLERIES

Europeans often guffaw at Vancouver's meager history, but that doesn't mean the city lacks intriguing museums. Rooted in Kitsilano's Vanier Park, the Museum of Vancouver (p111) is a one-stop shop for local history buffs and it often stages unusual exhibitions on themes such as downtown neon signs or regional skateboarding heritage. Just a few steps away, the Vancouver Maritime Museum (p111) illuminates the region's salty seafaring past and has plenty of scale models alongside its preserved original vessels.

You'll have to pull out a map to find some of the city's best museum attractions. The off-the-beaten-path Hastings Mill Store Museum (p110) is Vancouver's oldest building. Originally on Burrards Inlet's south shore, the 1865 structure survived the Great Fire before being floated to Kits in the 1930s. It now houses a menagerie of local artifacts and exhibits.

Since you're on the West Side, continue on to the UBC campus and the Museum of Anthropology at UBC (p119), regarded by many as the city's best cultural attraction. Recently expanded, it's a rich introduction to regional First Nations heritage, and it also explores intriguing cultures from around the world.

You can get an evocative history fix at the West End's Roedde House Museum (p42), where rooms at this colonial-era heritage home have been restored to their original Victorian grandeur. Across town, history of a more gritty nature lines the walls of the little Vancouver Police Centennial Museum (p67), where displays range from counterfeit currency to a mothballed mortuary room lined with preserved tissue samples.

Among local art institutions, the Vancouver Art Gallery (p42) is a stand-out. Emily Carr and EJ Hughes selections often grace the top floor, while other floors frequently exhibit local contemporary artists and blockbuster visiting shows. A few steps away, the new Bill Reid Gallery of Northwest Coast Art (p39) showcases the work of Canada's most revered Haida artist.

Alternatively, catch the next big thing at the free-entry gallery located at Emily Carr University (p94) on Granville Island. Then stroll up to South Granville and peruse the area's string of private galleries (p95) to see who's commanding the top market prices.

BEST GALLERY & MUSEUM SHOPS

> Bill Reid Gallery of Northwest Coast Art (p39)
> Museum of Anthropology at UBC (p119)
> Vancouver Art Gallery (p42)
> Vancouver Police Centennial Museum (p67)

BEST PRIVATE GALLERIES

> Bau-Xi Gallery (p104)
> Equinox Gallery (p104)
> Gallery of BC Ceramics (p95)
> JEM Gallery (p78)

Top left History display at the Museum of Vancouver (p111) **Above** Mortuary room at Vancouver Police Centennial Museum (p67)

PARKS & GARDENS

Tree-hugging outdoor fans will find plenty to salivate about on a trawl around Vancouver. Nature is rarely more than a few blocks from the end of your nose here, even in the heart of the city. But while the metropolis is ringed with tempting tree-lined slopes and dense, unkempt forests, there's also a diverse array of more-manicured outdoor attractions to please travelers. Wherever you end up, make sure you hit one of the city's rustic beach parks for a ravishing sunset view that's guaranteed to trigger some big love for Mother Nature.

The jewel in the city's natural crown is Stanley Park (p56) and you can expect to be subjected to a citizen's arrest if you fail to visit during your stay. North America's largest urban park space (yes, Central Park is rubbish), it's an ocean-fringed, 400-hectare jaw-dropper lined with 500,000 trees and crisscrossed with verdant trails. Most visitors stick to the smashing 8.8km seawall trail encircling the park – it's the kind of stroll that clears your mind and unknots any troubling muscles. Horticulture buffs should also visit the lovely rose and rhododendron gardens, while bird-spotters should wander around Lost Lagoon and outstare a beady-eyed heron or two.

The city's second most popular green attraction is over on the West Side. Queen Elizabeth Park (p102) was created on the site of an old quarry and the beautification process involved planting two large garden spaces with shrubs, flowers and trees from around the world. Bustling with visitors (and wedding parties) on summer days, its hilltop promontory offers one of Vancouver's most spectacular views: check the panorama of downtown's glass towers backed by snowcapped peaks. If inclement weather means you can't see further than the end of your lens, nip inside to the Bloedel Floral Conservatory (p102) for climate-controlled areas sans rain.

Since you're in this part of the city, consider hopping over to nearby VanDusen Botanical Garden (p103), Vancouver's leading privately owned outdoor attraction. The coiffured gardens are immaculate and you can get happily lost in the old-school maze. If you're visiting in winter, the gardens are strung with Christmas lights.

Heading out to UBC (p116) is also highly recommended. The giant university campus occupies an ocean-fringed Point Grey peninsula and is surprisingly stuffed with park and garden attractions. Consider a stroll along the dense, tree-lined trails of Pacific Spirit Regional Park (Map p117, C2) or hit the fascinating Botanical Garden (p118), complete with its canopy nature walk, before ending with a tranquility fix at the formal Japanese Nitobe Memorial Garden (p119), where you'll learn all about the symbolic representation of life though horticulture (who knew?).

The deep philosophy behind traditional gardens is also on display back in the city center at Chinatown's Dr Sun Yat-Sen Classical Chinese Garden (p66). The tour here is highly recommended, since it explains the detailed cultural reasons behind the placing of odd limestone formations and flare-roofed covered walkways. If you're on a budget, there's a smaller, free-entry park next door that follows similar rules.

Finally, wherever your green day out in Vancouver takes you, make sure you end it at one of the city's laid-back beach parks. Kitsilano Beach and nearby Jericho Beach (both p110) are idyllic spots to perch on a log, breathe in the gentle sea breeze and gaze at the glassy-calm ocean crowned by a pyrotechnic sunset.

BEST NATURE-HUGGING VIEWS
> Jericho Beach (p110)
> Kitsilano Beach (p111)
> Queen Elizabeth Park (p102)
> Stanley Park seawall (p56)

BEST PICNIC SPOTS
> Kitsilano Beach (p111)
> Lumberman's Arch or Second Beach, Stanley Park (p59)
> Third Beach, Stanley Park (p63)
> Vanier Park (p111)

Top left A verdant scene from Chinatown's Dr Sun Yat-Sen Classical Chinese Garden & Park (p66)

WATERFRONT WALKS

Vancouver's picturesque seawall allows calves-of-steel locals and hardy visitors to hike a highly enticing 22km stretch from downtown's Canada Place (p42) to Coal Harbour, around Stanley Park and along both sides of False Creek to Granville Island and then UBC. It's also a great cycling route.

Arguably a better way to approach the seawall is in bite-sized chunks. The short and easy stretch from Canada Place to Stanley Park takes you past diving floatplanes and intriguing public art – you can also stop for a beer at the Mill Marine Bistro (p52). Alternatively, the flat but long 8.8km trek encircling the park (p56) takes a few hours, but the ocean and mountain views are highly rewarding. From the English Bay (p42) side near Stanley Park, you'll pass busy beaches and eventually arrive on the fringes of Yaletown.

Many start their walk at Yaletown's David Lam Park (Map pp40–1, D7) for a stroll along the seawall lining the north side of False Creek, a busy inlet of bobbling boats. Keep your eyes peeled for artworks and birdlife along the shoreline as you pass under Cambie Bridge (Map pp40–1, E7) and alongside the former Expo '86 site, now forested with glass towers.

Science World (p66) marks the turn to the south side of False Creek. The final piece of the seawall puzzle, it was opened in early 2009. Continue westward and pass the giant Olympic Athletes Village (p78) on your left, followed on your right by Habitat Island. Topped with trees and shrubs, it's a new urban ecoreserve that invites nature – including cormorants, herons and falcons – back into the city.

Westward-bound, you'll next pass under the other end of Cambie Bridge and emerge at Stamps Landing. A crazy-paved seawall pocket of low-rise 1970s condos, it's very different to the swanky new towers across the water. Continue from here and you'll eventually reach Granville Island (p92). Stop here or recharge your batteries for an assault on the rest of the shoreline trail. The seawall curves northwest from here to Vanier Park (p111), the beaches of Kitsilano (p110) and, eventually, UBC (p120).

BEST WATERFRONT WALKS

> Canada Place to Stanley Park
> Kitsilano Beaches (p17)
> North False Creek
> South False Creek
> Stanley Park (p56)

BEST SEAWALL PITSTOPS

> Go Fish (p98)
> Granville Island's Public Market (p97)
> Mill Marine Bistro (p52)
> Raincity Grill (p49)
> Teahouse (p63)

Top left Canada Place (p42) as seen from across Burrard Inlet Above Go Fish (p98) on Granville Island

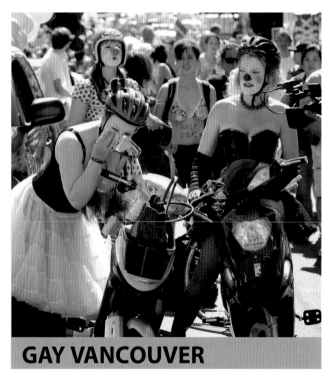

GAY VANCOUVER

You're standing on the sunny sidewalk with around 500,00 locals cheering and laughing while the smiling Dykes on Bikes zoom by, a procession of near-naked dance troupes shimmy past and dozens of slow-moving trucks topped with energetically gyrating young (and not-so-young) Vancouverites trundle into view. Welcome to the city's annual Pride Parade (p25), Canada's largest gay, lesbian, bisexual, transsexual (and everyone else) event and the prime exemplar of Vancouver's out-and-proud approach.

Centered on the West End's vibrant Davie St 'gayborhood,' Vancouver's GLBT scene is part of the mainstream here rather than a subculture – which means you can expect to see plenty of same-sex hand-holding as you stroll past the area's pink-painted bus shelters and rainbow-decal flags. You might also spot some dewy-eyed newlyweds: with Canada's 2005 legalization of same-sex marriage, Vancouver has become one of North America's leading destinations for gay travelers looking to tie the knot in an exotic locale.

If you're keen to tap the scene, do your homework before you arrive via the handy www.gayvancouver.net and www.superdyke.com websites, each stuffed with listings and resources. Once you're on the ground, pick up a free copy of *Xtra! West* newspaper to see what's on.

Among Davie St's stores and coffee shops, Little Sisters Book & Art Emporium (p44) is a good first stop. You can chat with the staff and rub shoulders with the locals or just stock up on 'specialist literature' before checking out the bulletin board of local happenings. You can also pick up a free copy of the glossy *Gay & Lesbian Business Association of BC* booklet for other area listings.

Naturally, Davie St is the center of the scene's happening nightlife. Ask the locals for suggestions – a chat-up line that might work – then consider the Fountainhead and PumpJack pubs (p51) as well as throbbing club venues such as Celebrities and Odyssey (both p54), where themed evenings can include teetering drag acts and well-oiled dancers in cages. And just in case you get lucky, make sure you're prepared: Denman St's Rubber Rainbow Condom Company (p44) opens at 7pm daily.

BEST GAY NIGHTLIFE HAUNTS

> 1181 (p51)
> Celebrities (p54)
> Fountainhead Pub (p51)
> Odyssey (p54)
> PumpJack Pub (p51)

BEST SPOT FOR WEDDING PHOTOS

> Jericho Beach (p110)
> Kitsilano Beach (p111)
> Pride Parade float (p25)
> Queen Elizabeth Park (p102)
> Stanley Park (p56)

Top left Enthusiastic partcipants at the annual Gay Pride Parade

GREEN VANCOUVER

Vancouver has a global reputation for green initiatives, most of which have sprung from the grassroots rather than at the government level. Wandering the city, you'll notice an outdoorsy populace that likes to celebrate the natural surroundings on foot, rollerblade or bicycle whenever possible (and in all weather). Many of the grinning, superfit West Coasters are active greenies – not surprising in a city where Greenpeace was founded (p113) and where David Suzuki, Canada's most revered ecoscientist, lives.

Apart from partaking in these activities and minimising the use of a car, you can start being green with your dining habits. **Ocean Wise** (www .vanaqua.org/oceanwise) encourages fish and shellfish suppliers to take eco-friendly and sustainable measures and also has listings of restaurants that support the idea. Check menus for symbols indicating Ocean Wise dishes. Some Ocean Wise eateries include: Bishop's (p113), Chambar (p47), Raincity Grill (p49), Fish House (p62) and West (p106).

A similar, smaller movement, the **Green Table Network** (www.greentable.net) helps identify restaurants that try to source all their supplies – not just seafood – from sustainable, mostly local sources. Peruse a copy of the Vancouver-written *100-Mile Diet: A Year of Local Eating* (p156) if you want to delve deeper into the issue, and seek to buy produce from farmers markets.

Hook up with green-minded locals at the lively **Green Drinks** (www .greendrinks.org) social event staged at the Steamworks Brewing Company (p73). Alternatively, pick up a copy of Vancouver's sustainable city mag, *Granville Magazine* (www.granvillemagazine.com). It reviews and analyzes green themes and concepts and has a lively website. *The Greater Vancouver Green Guide* (p156) offers additional tips on how to be 'green' during your visit as well as showcasing the region's best ecopractices and programs.

If you're staying awhile, perhaps splash out $30 on a **Green Zebra** (www .greenzebraguide.ca) coupon book. It's stuffed with hundreds of money-saving discounts and two-for-one deals at ecofriendly businesses throughout the region.

>BACKGROUND

The Hastings Mill Store Museum (p110) in Kitsilano is housed in Vancouver's oldest building

BACKGROUND

HISTORY

The First Nations residents of British Columbia (BC) had been living relatively peacefully off the area's tasty and abundant wildlife for thousands of years before 18th-century Russian, Spanish and British marine adventurers (including Captain James Cook) sailed in for an acquisitive look around. Mistaking Cook's crew for a boatful of transformed salmon in 1778, the locals were no match for the sailors' unexpected firepower and the interlopers soon began weighing up the possibilities of regional land claims.

But while international vessels poked around the fringes of the area for the next few years, it wasn't until 1792 that Captain George Vancouver breezed in to the densely tree-lined inner harbor…only to find that Spanish captains Valdez and Galiano had already been there and done that. The seafarers met cordially at what is now known as Spanish Banks (p120), possibly to plan the idyllic jogging trails that would one day crisscross the beach park, or more likely to size each other up. Legend has it that the crews shared navigational information before Captain Van sailed away, oblivious to the fact that the region would eventually house dozens of Tim Hortons coffee and donut outlets in a city named after him.

The economic possibilities of seemingly endless lumber supplies, trappable furry animals and oceans brimming with fish soon began to lure a trickle of adventurous pioneers to the area. The trickle became a tidal wave as commercial organizations such as the Hudson's Bay Company showed that money could be made and a new life could be had. Many people flooded in to escape the drudgery back home or, when the 1850s Gold Rush kicked in, to make their fortune.

By the early 1860s, thousands of giddy immigrants had arrived on ships from the Old World, prompting the British to officially seize control and claim the region as a crown colony. The names 'Not Quite Britain' and 'England Two: Son of England' were no doubt bandied about before 'British Columbia' was suggested and rubber-stamped.

At the time, settlers were emerging on the south bank of what later became Burrard Inlet. And, in 1867, an enterprising Yorkshireman called Jack Deighton – a talkative chap nicknamed 'Gassy' – opened a small bar to serve the thirsty workers of the nearby Hastings Sawmill. While early evening cocktails were rarely on the menu – gritty hard liquor and bloody fistfights were the more likely norms – the bar grew rapidly and triggered a rash of surrounding development that soon became known as 'Gastown.'

Later labeled Granville and then officially renamed Vancouver, this six-acre plot was the forerunner of the modern-day city. The area still houses some of the region's oldest buildings…along with a statue of 'Gassy' Jack perched atop a whiskey barrel.

Not everything went well for the fledgling city, though. While Vancouver soon reached a population of 1000 and was finally linked to the rest of the vast, emerging country by the Canadian Pacific Railway, it was almost completely destroyed in an 1886 blaze dubbed 'the Great Fire' (although it only lasted 20 minutes). A prompt rebuild followed and a new downtown began to take shape – this time a short distance away from the original settlement and using stone instead of wood for the most important structures.

Despite BC lumber flowing across the globe through the city's increasingly busy port (which quickly became Canada's largest), WWI and the Wall Street Crash triggered a slow and protracted depression in the region. Prosperity only returned when WWII sparked shipbuilding and armaments manufacturing, diversifying the city's economy away from logging.

Growing steadily through the 1950s and 1960s, Vancouver added a National Hockey League team (which still hasn't won the Stanley Cup), a full complement of dense residential neighborhoods and sprawling suburbs, and enough quality sushi eateries to feed the entire nation. The city has also gentrified away from its original gritty resource-and-industry base, with formerly grungy areas such as Granville Island, Coal Harbour and even skid-row Gastown now prettified and turned over to glass-tower developments and slick shops and restaurants.

HERITAGE-HUGGING CHINATOWN

Most of Chinatown's earliest residents were single men who came from southern China to work in sawmills, canneries and on railway construction. Within a few years, the ghetto they called home was a clamorous enclave of stores, theaters and rooming houses, with a seedy underbelly of brothels and opium dens. While Vancouverites of the time publicly condemned the area, many secretly sneaked in to partake of its illicit attractions.

In 1986 the transformation to modern metropolis was completed when the city hosted a highly successful Expo World's Fair, sparking a massive wave of development and adding the first of the mirrored skyscrapers that now define the downtown skyline. Hopes are high that the 2010 Olympic and Paralympic Winter Games, staged one year before Vancouver's official 125th birthday, will have a similar long-term positive effect on the city.

ART & ARCHITECTURE

Vancouver has a rich and varied art scene that sometimes seems hard to access. Despite its wealth of artists, galleries and events, there's a historic lack of synthesis here and often a parochial inability to work for a common cause. For visitors, this means you'll have to rub your chin reflectively and scratch beneath the city's surface a little to find its artsy pulse. Luckily, the effort is well worth it.

In the visual arts, photo-conceptualism is a regional specialty that attracts international recognition. Ask around and it won't be long before your hear the phrase 'Vancouver School,' which applies to sharp narrative imagery defined by leading local exponents such as Jeff Wall, Stan Douglas and Rodney Graham. One of the most famous works from the group is Douglas' *Every Building on 100 West Hastings*, a 3m-long panorama of mostly derelict but once-handsome Downtown Eastside buildings. The Vancouver Art Gallery (p42) has a giant permanent collection of this and other works and it stages regular exhibitions of its treasures.

It's not all about photos in Vancouver, though. Look out for the colorful stylized canvases of historic regional painters such as Emily Carr and EJ Hughes; the sci-fi style cartoons of Attila Richard Lukacs; the challenging abstracts of Jack Shadbolt; and both the traditional and modern First Nations works of Roy Henry Vickers or Brian Jungen – famed for transforming Nike running shoes into aboriginal masks.

Eclectic artist-run galleries have grown exponentially in the city in recent years, and the number of public-art installations now stretches to several hundred – plan a cost-free afternoon hunting down some of these using the online registry: www.city.vancouver.bc.ca/publicart. See p142 for a listing of some of these.

Architecture fans will also find plenty to gawp at on a wander around the city. Gastown, Chinatown and the wider Downtown Eastside are densely lined with landmark historic gems and faded, paint-peeled

SPANNING THE CITY

The postcard-hogging Lions Gate Bridge (Map p57, C1) is Vancouver's version of San Francisco's Golden Gate. Connecting downtown to the North Shore, it's named after a pair of snow-tipped regional peaks that resemble lion ears. Attractive but less grandiose, the lovely art-deco Burrard Bridge (Map pp40–1, B6) spans False Creek between downtown and Kitsilano and frames a spectacular view of the North Shore mountains. Complete with nautical flourishes and 'flaming' sentry beacons, it opened in 1932, when a Canadian air-force seaplane flew under the span to mark the occasion. It's a stunt that hasn't been tried since.

echoes of the past (look out for some smashing heritage neon signage still clinging on along E Hastings St). The city is also stuffed with cozy residential enclaves that define West Coast Craftsman construction in the colonial era. The West End and Kitsilano are especially well stocked with these great heritage homes – the former's Barclay Heritage Sq is particularly recommended for its row of preserved clapboard mansions, including Roedde House Museum (p42).

Grand, monumental architecture also studs the city's downtown core. The Vancouver Art Gallery (p42) was built as a courthouse by Francis Rattenbury, whose early-19th-century buildings define the colonial age across the province. Also keep your eyes peeled for a couple of art deco gems: the Marine Building (p45) is a stunningly ornate maritime-themed old skyscraper, while the interior of City Hall (p102) is a museum-piece reminder of streamlined design.

But the city's best buildings are not all old. The 1960s and 1970s saw the emergence of a local modernist post-and-beam approach, pioneered by Arthur Erickson, the city's most famous architect, who died in 2009. The movement – which became known around the world as 'Vancouver architecture' – is exemplified by city structures such as downtown's grand Provincial Law Courts and the newly renovated Museum of Anthropology at UBC (p119).

The defining architectural feature of today's cityscape is the shimmering translucent towers that prompted local author Douglas Coupland to coin the nickname 'City of Glass.' It's an approach you'll see in the rash of condo developments that forest the city and in the area's tallest new building. With a hotel on the bottom and condos up top, the 62-story sheer-glass **Shangri-La tower** (Map pp40-1, D3; 1128 W Georgia St) opened in 2009. It's a neck-cracking 201m high, which means its top floors are frequently hidden in the clouds on foggy days.

FURTHER READING

Vancouver has a lively literary heritage and some recommended landmark works of fiction to get you in the mood before you arrive. There's also a wealth of nonfiction tomes for those who want to do their homework before stepping off the plane. With Vancouver boasting the highest proportion of book readers in Canada, the city's One Book, One Vancouver campaign is, not surprisingly, wildly successful. A giant book club deploying a single volume with a local tie, the annual campaign sparks mass reading, heated discussions and literary events across the region. Previous selections have included *The Corporation*, *Stanley Park* and 2009's ski-themed *Crazy Canucks*.

100-Mile Diet: A Year of Local Eating (JB Mackinnon and Alisa Smith, 2008) Highly readable real-life depiction of the trials and tribulations endured by a Vancouver couple trying to source all their food – right down to the salt on their table – from the local area.

City of Glass (Douglas Coupland, 2000) Brilliantly quirky, picture-packed alternative guidebook of musings and observations on contemporary Vancouver from the city's fave living author.

Crazy Canucks: Canada's Legendary Ski Team (Janet Love Morrison, 2008) True-life story of the pioneering skiers who shook the Euro-dominated world of international competition in the 1970s.

Fresh: Seasonal Recipes Made with Local Foods (John Bishop, 2007) A celebration of locavore BC produce and its dedicated growers, this sumptuous 100-recipe book underlines Bishop's credentials as the city's leading sustainable restaurateur.

Greater Vancouver Green Guide (various authors, 2006) Handy pocket-sized guidebook to environmental programs and initiatives in the city and beyond. A good tome for those who want to be green as much as possible during their visit.

History of Metropolitan Vancouver (Chuck Davis, 2007) A comprehensive and highly readable exploration of city history from Vancouver's leading popular historian. Packed with stories and unexpected anecdotes.

Hope in Shadows: Stories and Photographs of Vancouver's Downtown Eastside (various authors, 2008) Evocative images and stories by Eastside residents depicting the heart and soul of the troubled downtown community.

J-Pod (Douglas Coupland, 2006) One of a string of novels by Coupland exploring the slacker-flavored ennui of modern-day life among his usual cast of twenty-something misfits.

Jade Peony (Wayson Choy, 1995) A searing portrayal of growing up in a Vancouver Chinese immigrant family in the 1930s. Evocative and touching.

Necromancer (William Gibson, 1984) The legendary sci-fi author has called Vancouver home for many years and his seminal novel launched the genre of bleak, high-tech neoreality – think *The Matrix*.

Public Art in Vancouver: Angels Among Lions (John Steil and Aileen Stalker, 2009) Excellent guidebook detailing the wealth of hundreds of public artworks dotted around the city's streets. Perfect for artsy-type visitors.

Runaway: Diary of a Street Kid (Evelyn Lau, 2001) A 14-year-old honor student when she ran away from home, Lau's personal experience becomes the basis for this novelization of a dangerous life on the streets.

Saltwater City (Paul Yee, 2006) Illuminating and well-illustrated retelling of the often-tumultuous history of Vancouver's Chinese community, one of the largest and most intriguing in North America.

Stanley Park (Timothy Taylor, 2002) Fictionalizing modern-day Vancouver through a story fusing the life of a local chef with the park's dark secrets.

Vancouver Cooks (Jamie Maw, 2004) Fifty Vancouver-area chefs come together to offer their favorite menus plus more than 100 recipes giving a true taste of the region and its cosmopolitan, sometimes eclectic dining approaches.

Vancouver Remembered (Michael Kluckner, 2006) Generously illustrated and highly browsable coffee-table book recollecting the sights and stories of yesteryear Vancouver. A heavy tome but a good gift book for nostalgia buffs.

Vancouver Stories (various authors, 2005) An evocative series of pithy short stories about the city by a galaxy of writers including Douglas Coupland, Alice Munro, Ethel Wilson, Malcolm Lowry, William Gibson and Timothy Taylor.

Vij's: Elegant and Inspired Indian Cuisine (Vikram Viz and Meeru Dhalwala, 2006) Mirroring the authors' celebrated Indian restaurant, the recipes here offer an exciting twist on the subcontinent's traditional meals, giving away the secrets to some of Vij's mouthwatering dishes.

Wreck Beach (Carellin Brooks, 2007) A revealing history of Vancouver's famed naturist beach, with plenty of colorful stories and some grainy black-and-white images.

FILMS

Canada's 'Hollywood North' has been cranking out movies and TV shows for several decades, but the city usually doubles anonymously for generic American destinations. The locals aren't fooled, though, and you'll sometimes hear them chuckling at screenings as they watch Stanley Park standing in for Central Park or the Vancouver Art Gallery doubling as a city hall. Check out these shows and films shot in or around the city…then hunt down the sets when you hit town.

6th Day (directed by Roger Spottiswoode, 2000) This Arnie action flick made wide use of city locations, including transforming the Public Library into the headquarters of a dastardly cybernetics corporation (is there any other type?).

Catwoman (directed by Pitof, 2004) Arguably the worst big-budget film ever shot in the city – Halle Berry likes to pretend this one never happened. Time for a sequel? We think not.

Delicate Art of Parking (directed by Trent Carlson, 2003) A mockumentary about a Vancouver parking officer and the hassles he encounters ticketing irate motorists.

Elf (directed by John Favreau, 2003) No, the North Pole scenes were not shot on Grouse Mountain, but this Will Ferrell yuletide trifle used downtown's Hudson's Bay department store for interiors. You can ride the elevators just like Buddy…

LIGHTS, CAMERA, ACTION

The website of the **BC Film Commission** (www.bcfilmcommission.com) is the first stop for anyone interested in breaking into the biz on their Vancouver visit. The site gives the weekly low-down on what's filming and who's in the cast and crew, and provides contact information for productions seeking extras. Time to start rehearsing that Robert De Niro speech from *Taxi Driver*…

Fantastic Four (directed by Tim Story, 2005) The true story of radiation-exposed young astronauts using their superpowers to defeat baddie Doctor Victor Von Doom. Well, maybe not *that* true…

I, Robot (directed by Alex Proyas, 2004) Various locations were deployed around the region, including New Westminster's 'antique alley' which, of course, became Chicago of the not-too-distant future.

Mount Pleasant (directed by Ross Weber, 2007) Three couples from Vancouver's SoMa find their lives tangling in a mess of obsession and tragedy when a child finds a discarded junkie needle in her garden. Should have been a musical.

On the Corner (directed by Nathaniel Geary, 2003) A gritty look at life in Vancouver's heroin-plagued Downtown Eastside that follows a young man drawn into the worlds of addiction and prostitution.

Twilight: New Moon (directed by Chris Weitz, 2009) Filming the trials and tribulations of vampire love turned the city into *Twilight* central for teenage fans in early 2009, with star sightings and near-stalkings the order of the day.

Smallville (various directors, from 2001) The early struggles of a young-adult Superman was filmed at multiple locations across the city, from the Art Gallery to Kitsilano.

X-Files: I Want to Believe (directed by Chris Carter, 2008) The humdrum big-movie sequel returned to Vancouver, where its multiseason TV show was filmed from 1993 onwards. This time, star David Duchovny was careful not to complain about the rain.

X-Men (directed by Bryan Singer, 2000) All three movies in the mutant-hero franchise were shot in and around the city, with stars such as Ian McKellan and Hugh Jackman frequently popping up in local restaurants to scare the locals.

DIRECTORY

TRANSPORTATION

If Vancouver's efforts to continually upgrade it's transportation are any guide, the world's most livable city aims to stay that way. The downtown area and its environs are very foot-friendly.

ARRIVAL & DEPARTURE

AIR

Vancouver International Airport (code YVR; ☎ 604-207-7077; www.yvr.ca) is the West Coast's main hub for airlines from across Canada, the US and international locales. It's in Richmond, a 13km/30-minute drive southeast of downtown Vancouver. Linked to the main airport by shuttle bus, the airport's South Terminal services only British Columbia flights operated by smaller operators.

Getting To/From the Airport

The new 16-station **Canada Line** (☎ 604-953-3333; www.canadaline.com) rapid-transit train runs from the airport into downtown. The full trip to Waterfront station (Map pp40–1; F3) takes 25 minutes. At time of writing, fares to or from the airport were expected to be at least $7 for an adult ticket.

The **Vancouver Airporter** (☎ 604-946-8866, 800-668-3141; www.yvrairporter.com; one way/return $13.75/21.50; ✆ 5.30am-11.45pm, reduced hrs in winter) shuttle bus

delivers passengers to major city-center hotels in about 40 minutes. Pay the driver or buy a ticket at the desk on level 2 of the airport.

Cabs charge up to $35 for the 30-minute trip from the airport to downtown. Follow the airport signs for pick-up points.

Floatplane & Helicopter

Several handy floatplane services swoop into Vancouver's downtown harbor near Canada Place (p42) from Vancouver Island and beyond. Operators include **Harbour Air Seaplanes** (☎ 604-274-1277, 800-665-0212; www.harbour-air.com) and

Recommended Modes of Transportation

	Downtown	Stanley Park	Gastown & Chinatown
Downtown	n/a	walk 15mins	walk 10mins
Stanley Park	walk 10mins	n/a	walk 10mins
Gastown & Chinatown	walk 10mins	bus 15mins	n/a
SoMa	bus 15mins	bus 30mins	bus 10mins
Commercial Drive	SkyTrain 10mins	bus and SkyTrain 30mins	bus 15mins
Granville Island	bus 10mins	bus 20mins	bus 15mins
Fairview & Sth Granville	bus or Canada Line 10mins	bus 20mins	bus 15mins
Kitsilano	bus 15mins	bus 20mins	bus 25mins
UBC	bus 35mins	bus 1hr	bus 40mins

West Coast Air (☎ 604-606-6888, 800-347-2222; www.westcoastair.com). **Helijet** (☎ 604-273-4688, 800-665-4354; www.helijet.com) operates a rival helicopter service from the terminal (Map p65, B1) on the east side of the SeaBus ferry terminal.

BUS

The main intercity bus terminal is at **Pacific Central Station** (Map p65, C6; ☎ 604-661-0325; 1150 Station St). Long-distance Canadian bus services are provided by **Greyhound Canada** (☎ 800-661-8747; www.greyhound.ca) and, from the US, by **Greyhound** (☎ 800-231-2222; www.greyhound.com). **Pacific Coach Lines** (☎ 604-662-7575, 800-661-1725; www.pacificcoach.com) buses also service routes to Victoria and Whistler from here. In addition, **Quick Coach Lines** (☎ 604-940-4428,

800-665-2122; www.quickcoach.com) operates an express shuttle from Seattle (downtown and Sea-Tac International Airport).

TRAIN

Trains trundle in from across Canada and the USA northwest at **Pacific Central Station** (Map p65, C6; ☎ 604-661-0325; 1150 Station St). Canadian services are provided by **VIA Rail** (☎ 888-842-7245; www.viarail.ca), while US services are provided by **Amtrak** (☎ 800-872-7245; www.amtrak.com). Intercity buses also operate from the station and the Main St-Science World SkyTrain station is a short walk away.

VISA

Visitors from Scandinavia, European Community countries and

SoMa	Commercial Drive	Granville Island	Fairview & Sth Granville	Kitsilano	UBC
bus 15mins	SkyTrain 10mins	bus 10mins	bus or Canada Line 10mins	bus 10mins	bus 15mins
bus 15mins	SkyTrain 10mins	bus 10mins	bus 20mins	bus 15mins	bus 35mins
bus 10mins	bus 15mins	bus 15mins	bus 15mins	bus 20mins	bus 40mins
n/a	bus 10mins	bus 20mins	bus 10mins	bus 25mins	bus 40mins
bus 10mins	n/a	bus 30mins	bus 20mins	bus 40mins	bus 45mins
bus 20mins	bus 30mins	n/a	walk 15mins	walk 10mins	bus 35mins
bus 10mins	bus 20mins	walk 10mins	n/a	bus 10mins	bus 30mins
bus 25mins	bus 40mins	walk 10mins	bus 10mins	n/a	bus 20mins
bus 40mins	bus 45mins	bus 35mins	bus 30mins	bus 20mins	n/a

many Commonwealth nations do not need visas to enter Canada, but citizens of dozens of other countries do. Check the website of **Citizenship & Immigration Canada** (www.cic.gc.ca) for the latest requirements. At the border, you may be asked to show proof of sufficient funds or evidence of onward or departure travel. From June 2009, all US citizens now need a passport to get back home across the border.

GETTING AROUND
It's a breeze getting around Vancouver, with SkyTrain, Canada Line, bus and SeaBus public transportation options available. All of these services are overseen by **TransLink** (☎ 604-953-3333; www .translink.bc.ca).

TRAVEL PASSES
An all-day, all-zone transit pass covering TransLink services costs $9/7 for an adult/child. It's available at local stores such as Safeway, 7-11 and London Drugs (look for the blue FairDealer sign), as well as at SkyTrain station ticket machines.

PUBLIC TRANSPORTATION
A ticket bought on any **TransLink** (☎ 604-953-3333; www.translink .bc.ca) service is valid for up to 90 minutes of travel across the entire network, depending on the zone you intend to travel in. One-zone tickets cost $2.50/1.75 for an adult/child, two-zone tickets are $3.75/2.50 and three-zone tickets cost $5/3.50. If you're traveling after 6:30pm or on weekends or

GREENER WAYS TO VANCOUVER

Flying to Vancouver is a long-haul trek for many travelers and, short of teleportation, it's not easy to reach the West Coast any other way. However, if you're traveling across Canada or coming from the USA, consider taking the train. The 'slow travel' approach will add time to your trip but the rewards of seeing the beautiful land you're passing through are immense – and the journey will be far more enjoyable than the hassles of airline travel. See p160 for information on train operators servicing Vancouver.

holidays, all fares are classed as one-zone trips.

SeaBus aquatic shuttle services operate every 10 to 30 minutes throughout the day, taking 12 minutes to cross Burrard Inlet between downtown's Waterfront station (Map pp40–1, F3) and North Vancouver's Lonsdale Quay. Tickets must be purchased in advance from vending machines on either side of the route. Services depart Waterfront between 6:15am and 1:20am Monday to Saturday (8am to 11:15pm Sunday). Vessels are bike friendly and wheelchair accessible.

Local **buses** use on-board fare machines, so exact change (or more) is required and no change is given. The network is extensive in the downtown area and many

buses have bike racks; most are also wheelchair accessible.

The **SkyTrain** rapid-transit network consists of Expo Line and Millennium Line routes. Trains depart every two to eight minutes between 5am and 1:15am Monday to Friday (6am to 12:30am Saturday, 7am to 11:30pm Sunday). Tickets must be purchased from station vending machines (change is given for bills up to $20) before boarding.

The new 16-station **Canada Line** (www.canadaline.com) rapid-transit train system links the airport, Richmond and downtown Vancouver. At time of research, a $2 premium above the three-zone transit fare was anticipated for the airport branch line.

BOAT

Aquabus Ferries (☎ 604-689-5858; www.theaquabus.com; adult/child from $3/1.50) runs mini vessels (some big enough to carry bikes) between the foot of Hornby St (Map pp40–1, B6) and Granville Island. They also service additional points around False Creek, including Science World (Map p65, B6). Service times vary by season but the boats run every few minutes from dawn to dusk in summer.

False Creek Ferries (☎ 604-684-7781; www.granvilleislandferries.bc.ca; adult/child from $3/1.50) operates a similar Granville Island service, this time from the Aquatic Centre (Map pp40–1, B6), plus ports of call around False Creek. Both operators offer same-price day passes: adult/child $14/8.

STREETCAR

The track of the **Downtown Historic Railway** (☎ 604-665-3903; www.trams .bc.ca) was undergoing repairs at the time of research. It normally runs from south of Granville Island (Map p93, A5) to Science World (Map p65, B6).

TAXI

Flagging a cab on main streets in downtown shouldn't take too long, but it's easier if your hotel calls you one. Vancouver has one of the world's largest hybrid-vehicle taxi fleets, so you'll likely be traveling green. Meters start at $2.73, then add $1.58 per kilometer.

Black Top & Checker Cabs (☎ 604-731-1111)
Vancouver Taxi (☎ 604-871-1111)
Yellow Cab (☎ 604-681-1111)

PRACTICALITIES
BUSINESS HOURS

Banks 9am-5pm Mon-Fri, some branches 9am-noon Sat
Post offices 9:30am-5:30pm Mon-Fri, some branches 10am-4pm Sat
Pubs & bars noon-11pm, later on weekends
Restaurants breakfast from 7am, lunch 11:30am-2:30pm, dinner 5-10pm
Shops 10am-6pm Mon-Sat, noon-5pm Sun

CHILDREN

Vancouver is very kid friendly and there are plenty of sights and activities here to tire out the little sprogs. Pick up a free copy of the *Kids' Guide Vancouver* flyer from racks around town or check www .kidsvancouver.com and www.find familyfun.com to see what's on.

The city's top two family-friendly educational attractions are Science World (p66), which offers a frenzy of hands-on activities aimed especially at under-10s, and the Vancouver Aquarium (p60), where there's a broader range of animal-spotting shenanigans for all ages.

Stanley Park has many other attractions (see p58). Check out the Miniature Railway and Children's Farmyard, but there's also sandy Third Beach, the Second Beach swimming pool and the shoreline water park near Lumberman's Arch. There's also a playground near the pool.

Kids who like to run around (is there any other type?) should get a kick out of the BC Sports Hall of Fame (p39), where there is lots to keep them occupied. The HR Macmillan Space Centre (p110) has plenty of high-tech touch-screen activities.

More-bookish youngsters will enjoy Kidsbooks (p112), a giant utopia of children's tomes that hosts readings and events. Granville Island's Kids Market (p95) is a

BEST KID-FRIENDLY FESTIVALS
> Celebration of Light (p25)
> Pacific National Exhibition (p26)
> Santa Claus Parade (p28)
> Vancouver International Children's Festival (p24)

two-level hall lined with toy, craft and candy stores. There's another free water park nearby. If you need to lure them away, offer a trip on one of the tiny ferries (p162) that ply the waters around the island.

DISCOUNTS
Aside from the triple-museum **Explore Pass** (p111), the **See Vancouver Card** (☎ 877-295-1157; www.seevancou vercard.com; 2-/3-/5-day adult $119/149/219, child $79/99/149) covers entry to more than 50 area attractions and is good value if you intend to hit as many sights as possible in a short time frame.

Many attractions offer concessionary entry for seniors and students (you may be asked for ID), while child discounts are often divided between higher youth rates (typically for ages 12 to 17 years) and lower child rates (for under-12s).

EMERGENCIES
Persistent street begging is a problem for Vancouver visitors:

just say 'Sorry' and keep walking if you're not interested and want to be polite. A small, hard-core group of scam artists also trawls the city preying on tourists by asking for money to get home. These mostly male scammers work the downtown core every day and never seem to make it 'home.'

In an emergency, dial ☎ 911 for police, fire and ambulance services. Other useful numbers:
Police (nonemergency) ☎ 604-717-3321
Poison Info Line ☎ 604-682-5050
Rape Crisis Centre ☎ 604-255-6344, 877-392-7583

HOLIDAYS
New Year's Day January 1
Good Friday & Easter Monday late March to mid-April
Victoria Day third Monday in May
Canada Day July 1
BC Day first Monday in August
Labour Day first Monday in September
Thanksgiving second Monday in October
Remembrance Day November 11
Christmas Day December 25
Boxing Day December 26

INTERNET
Among Vancouver's handful of internet cafes try **Star Internet** (Map pp40-1, B2; ☎ 604-685-4645; 1690 Robson St; per hr $2; ☀ 24hr) or head to the **Vancouver Public Library** (Map pp40-1, E5; ☎ 604-331-3600; 350 W Georgia St; per 30min free; ☀ 10am-9pm Mon-Thu, 10am-6pm Fri & Sat, noon-5pm Sun) for

nonmember terminals and free wi-fi (request an access code). In addition, coffee shops across the city increasingly offer free wi-fi.

Useful websites include:

Discover Vancouver (www.discovervancou ver.com) General visitors' guide.

Miss 604 (www.miss604.com) Insider's blog on all things Vancouver.

Only Magazine (www.onlymagazine.ca) Local alternative online zine.

Tourism Vancouver (www.tourismvancou ver.com) Official visitor site.

Urban Diner (www.urbandiner.ca) Listings and reviews covering area restaurants.

Vancouver 2010 (www.vancouver2010.com) Official site for the 2010 Olympics.

MONEY

Vancouver is one of Canada's priciest cities and average daily costs can be around $200 to $300 for accommodation, meals, transport and activities. It's not hard to spend more than that if you throw in a fancy meal and a stay in a swank sleepover. Typical costs include: pint of beer $6, dinner for two $60, double room in hotel $150, and one-day ski pass $42 to $56.

You can exchange currency at main bank branches, which often charge less than the bureaux de change dotted around the city. The **Vancouver Bullion & Currency Exchange** (Map pp40-1, E4; ☎ 604-685-1008; 800 W Pender St; ☼ 9am-5pm Mon-Fri) usually offers the city's best rates.

NEWSPAPERS

Georgia Straight (www.straight.com) Leading listings paper.

Province (www.theprovince.com) Daily tabloid.

Tyee (www.thetyee.ca) Online Vancouver news alternative.

Vancouver Sun (www.vancouversun.com) Main city daily.

Westender (www.westender.com) Quirky downtown community newspaper.

Xtra! West (www.xtra.ca) Free gay and lesbian paper.

ORGANIZED TOURS

It's not hard to find a bus tour in Vancouver, but check out the following for something a little less touristy:

A Wok Around Chinatown (☎ 604-736-9508; www.awokaround.com; tours $90; ☼ 10am Fri-Mon) Culinary- and history-themed four-hour trawl around old Chinatown (includes lunch and attractions).

Architectural Institute of BC (☎ 604-683-8555, ext 333; www.aibc.ca; tours $5; ☼ 1pm Tue-Sat Jul & Aug) Six highly recommended architecture tours covering areas from Yaletown to the West End.

Edible BC (☎ 604-812-9660; www .edible-britishcolumbia.com; tours from $49) Offering lip-smacking culinary-themed tours of Granville Island, Commercial Drive and Chinatown, plus wider-afield treks to the Southern Gulf Islands.

Gastown Historic Walking Tours (☎ 604-683-5650; www.gastown.org; tours free; ☼ 2pm mid-Jun–Aug) Illuminating the history and architecture of Vancouver's birthplace. Departs from 'Gassy' Jack statue.

Harbour Air Seaplanes (☎ 604-233-3505, 800-665-0212; www.harbourair.com; tours from $99; ☑ times vary, year-round) Spectacular 20-30-minute scenic flights around the mountain-ringed harbor that show just how stunning Vancouver's natural setting is. The take-off and landing are equally memorable.

Orpheum Theatre (☎ 604-665-3050; 884 Granville St; tours adult/child $10/5; ☑ Jul & Aug) The city's sumptuous baroque playhouse offers an entertaining but little-known 90-minute backstage tour.

TELEPHONE
US travelers can usually use their cell phones in Canada but should check with their service provider for tariffs. Visitors from other countries will probably be out of luck, unless their phone is a tri-band model operating on GSM 1900 and other frequencies. Public telephones are increasingly rare on Vancouver's streets but discount phonecards are widely available – local phone company **Telus** (www.telus.com) offers a range of reliable cards available at area convenience stores.

COUNTRY & CITY CODES
Country code ☎ 1
City codes ☎ 604, ☎ 778

USEFUL PHONE NUMBERS
Local and long-distance Canada and US directory assistance ☎ 411
Long-distance Canada and US direct-dial access code ☎ 1 + area code

International directory assistance ☎ 0
International direct dial access code ☎ 011 + country code

TIPPING
Following typical North American protocols, these tipping standards usually apply:
Bartenders 15% or $1 per drink
Hotel maids $2–5 per night
Hotel porters $2 per item
Restaurants 15%
Taxis 10%
Valet parking $5

TOURIST INFORMATION
Tourism Vancouver Tourist Information Centre (Map pp40-1, E3; ☎ 604-683-2000; www.tourismvancouver.com; 200 Burrard St, downtown; ☑ 8:30am-6pm Jun-Aug, 8:30am-5pm Mon-Sat Sep-May; Ⓜ Waterfront) offers free maps, visitor guides and half-price theater tickets, plus accommodation and tour bookings. There's also a seasonal booth near the Vancouver Art Gallery entrance and two additional counters at the airport.

TRAVELERS WITH DISABILITIES
Vancouver is an accessible city. On arrival at the airport, vehicle-rental agencies can provide pre-arranged cars that have hand-controls, while the Airporter (p159) shuttle bus can arrange transportation to Vancouver's ma-

jor hotels. Accessible cabs are also throughout the city, on request.

All **TransLink** (www.translink.bc.ca) SkyTrain and SeaBus services and most transit buses are wheelchair accessible. Check the website for information on accessible transport options. Check for other accessible-transport information in Vancouver and throughout Canada at www .accesstotravel.gc.ca.

Additional resources:

BC Coalition of People with Disabilities (☎ 604-875-0188; www.bccpd.bc.ca) Programs and support for people with disabilities.

Canadian National Institute for the Blind (☎ 604-431-2121; www.cnib.ca) Support and services for the visually impaired.

Western Institute for the Deaf and Hard of Hearing (☎ 604-736-7391; www.widhh .com) Interpreter services and resources for the hearing impaired.

>INDEX

See also separate subindexes for See (p174), Shop (p175), Eat (p173), Drink (p173) and Play (p174).

INDEX

000 map pages

🄯 SHOP

000 map pages